NICE
UNCOVERED

Walks Through the
Secret Heart of a Historic City

JEANNE OLIVER

Book cover and interior layout design:
Shabbir Hussain, access.ideas@yahoo.com

ISBN: 9780578359366

CONTENTS

ABOUT THIS BOOK

Like most newcomers to Nice, I was initially so enchanted by the seaside, it was hard to pull myself away and explore the city beyond the Promenade des Anglais. Over the years a different, subtler beauty emerged. The sun-dappled streets of Vieux Nice seemed to whisper secrets of a tangled past. Exquisite Belle Epoque palaces along the boulevards of Cimiez conjured up an era of balls and horse-drawn carriages. Majestic Art Deco buildings heralded a new age of ease and elegance as Nice gracefully adjusted to modernity.

As I wandered Nice's neighborhoods, I wondered how and why Nice developed as it did. What are the stories behind the many parks and monuments, churches and landmarks? In researching this book, I learned to see the city in a new way and that is what I hope to share with readers.

These seven essential walks cover all the sights of interest to first-time visitors as well as previously obscure sights that will surprise even long-term residents. Which walks you decide to take and in what order depends on your time and interest, but they're organized more or less chronologically to trace Nice's urban development. Each walk takes from 1½ to 3½ hours, possibly longer if museum visits are included.

INTRODUCTION

Between snow-capped mountains and an azure sea lies Nice, the queen of the French Riviera. The venerable old city began as a tiny hill settlement and evolved to become a sun-soaked metropolis of gardens and parks, splendid sea views, architectural masterpieces and richly decorated churches. Along the way, the city battled war and pestilence, poverty and occupation. Yet its indomitable spirit prevailed.

The *Niçois* spirit is forged from its identity as a Mediterranean city that is both part of and apart from France. Although ruled by northern Italy for centuries, France never fully accepted the situation. Every so often a French ruler would swoop down to grab what they could until Nice swung back to Italy. As a result, Nice absorbed influences from both countries without fully belonging to either. Even the local language, *Nissart*, is not quite French and not quite Italian

Perhaps because its national identity was perpetually in flux, Nice became comfortably multicultural, at least as compared to its neighbors. Most of the time the city was a welcoming environment for Jews who were being persecuted elsewhere in Europe. When it became clear in the late 18th century that rich northern Europeans were looking for sunny, healthy spots to combat respiratory illnesses, that spirit of openness became a business plan.

By the time Nice passed definitively to France in 1860 foreign tourists were a cornerstone of the local economy. Their tastes determined the face of the city. The British wanted a seaside stroll and so built the Promenade des Anglais. When Queen Victoria chose Cimiez as her holiday spot, chic hotels for trendsetting notables replaced sleepy farms and pastures. Visitors needed greenery and so parks arose throughout the city. Entire neighborhoods, such as the Quartier des Musiciens, were developed to house wealthy foreigners.

As Nice became ever more glamorous and exciting, its cultural life flourished. Painters, filmmakers, writers, philosophers, composers and architects found Nice a congenial place to contemplate and create. Matisse, Dufy, Chekhov, Berlioz and Nietzsche are long gone but their creative spirit is reflected in Nice's many public sculptures and buildings of outstanding artistic quality.

As you stroll Nice's neighborhoods you'll discover Nice's struggles and triumphs, its fervent faith and equally fervent pride in its traditions. Behind the iconic buildings and ancient streets lie stories of crooks and kings, saints and sinners, heroes, lovers and fighters. Together they wove a rich tapestry just waiting to be discovered.

NICE NEIGHBORHOOD MAP

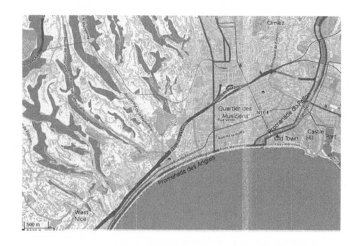

HISTORY

A Tale of Two Hills

Nice's story begins around the 3rd century BC when ancient Greeks from Phocaea established a colony on the Colline du Chateau, probably supplanting the Ligurian population. Little is known about this early settlement except that it established trade links with another Greek colony, *Massalia*, now Marseilles. The colony became known as *Nikaïa* possibly after *Nike*, the Greek word for victory. Although no remnants of the Greek settlement remain, it was these ancient settlers who introduced olive trees and grape vines to the region.

Romans swept through the region in the 2nd century BC and established a military outpost, Cemenelum, on top of Cimiez hill. Strategically located along the Via Julia between Spain and Italy, Cemenelum became the Roman capital of the Alpes Maritimes province. The population was about 10,000 people which included the Ligurian tribes under Roman authority. Roman baths and an amphitheater on Cimiez hill are vivid reminders of the Roman presence.

Meanwhile, Christianity arrived in the region. Two Christian martyrs—Saint Pontius and Saint Reparata—left an enduring mark on Nice's spiritual life. Saint Pontius was beheaded in 257AD under the Emperor Valerian. Five centuries later the influential Saint Pons abbey was built on the site of his burial spot. Saint Reparata was martyred in Palestine in the 3rd century and, according to legend, floated to Nice in a boat accompanied by angels. Nice's cathedral Sainte Réparate is dedicated to her.

By the time of Rome's fall in 476, there was enough of a Christian community to support the construction of two churches. Both Cimiez and the Colline du Chateau contain remnants of these early churches that date from the 5th century. It's supposed that there was also a Jewish community that dated from the 3rd century.

After the Fall

The fall of Rome marked the beginning of a high-conflict era in Nice. First there was the Visigoth invasion. Cimiez could not be defended and was gradually abandoned. The Ostrogoths arrived only to be driven out when Nice became part of the Eastern Roman empire in 550.

After the Lombard conquest of Nice in 641 Nice became part of Liguria and recognized Genoa as its capital. Although interrupted by devastating Saracen raids in the 9th century and then a period of domination by the hated Counts of Provence, Nice remained closely allied with Genoa. Finally in 1229 the Provencal Count Raymond Berenger V conquered the city.

Expansion

During the 13th century Nice's population expanded and its economy strengthened, largely due to the burgeoning salt trade. Population pressures pushed inhabitants down from the walled Colline du Chateau to the eastern part of Vieux

Nice where the Franciscans built a church and monastery. Walls were built to protect the settlers.

The Beginning of Savoy Rule

Matters took a turn for the worse in the 14th century. The bubonic plague ripped through town from 1347 to 1348, then again in 1359 and 1373, cutting the population in half. No sooner had the plague receded than a new threat arose when the Provencal Countess Joanna died without a successor. A civil war erupted and Nice, unluckily, backed the wrong faction. The town was forced to turn to Count Amadeus VII of Savoy for protection. Nice voluntarily became part of the House of Savoy in 1388, an event that determined the city's development for almost five centuries.

Nice flourished under the new management. The old nobility fled to Provence and a new order of ennobled merchants rose to power. Along with neighboring Villefranche, Nice became Savoy's only seaport and grew prosperous again from the salt trade. The Savoy dukes protected their new possession by fortifying the Colline du Chateau. A Jewish community developed composed of immigrants fleeing persecution elsewhere in France. Some settled on rue Benoit Bunico in Vieux Nice; others settled around the Port.

The Siege

The early 16th century ushered in a period of turbulence, mainly because Savoy became enmeshed in wars between the King of France, François I, and Emperor Charles V. A peace deal between the warring parties was negotiated in Nice in 1538 but it fizzled. As Savoy was allied with Charles V, Nice came under attack from a Franco-Turk alliance in 1543. During the assault, a washerwoman, Catherine Segurane, allegedly climbed on top the town's ramparts, seized a Turkish flag and wiped her bottom with it. The horrified Turks fled, saving the fortified Colline du Chateau, but Vieux Nice was pillaged before the attackers were driven out.

The siege was a seminal event in Nice's history. Catherine Segurane became a popular local heroine, symbolizing the fiercely independent Nice spirit. Cannonballs from the assault are displayed (triumphantly?) in and around Vieux Nice. Following the devastating assault, the Savoy dukes decided to turn the Colline du Chateau into a fortified citadel. New towers surrounded the citadel and civilians were sent to Vieux Nice.

The Age of Baroque

The population increase ushered in a golden age for the Old Town. Making Nice a *port franc* in 1612, in which port taxes were abolished, boosted trade and commerce. Flush with cash, rich merchants built residences such as the Palais Lascaris or Palais Caïs de Pierlas in the Old Town. They also financed the construction or expansion of numerous churches including the venerable Cathedral of Sainte Réparate.

The building spree that lasted from the mid-17th to late 18th century coincided with the great era of baroque architecture. Under pressure from the Protestant Reformation, the Catholic church introduced this highly theatrical, richly decorated style that aimed to surprise and awe churchgoers. The lighting was dramatic, the colors vibrant, and the eye drawn upwards toward heaven.

Originating in Italy the style was quickly adopted in Nice and applied to both sacral and civil structures. Vieux Nice contains a profusion of stunning baroque churches that mix Genoese and Piedmont styles. Eglise du Gesù, Chapelle de la Miséricorde, L'Eglise de l'Annonciation, and the lavish Cathedral Sainte Réparate are the most splendid examples of baroque style. The Palais Lascaris and Palais Corvésy show how powerful families used baroque style to display their wealth.

The End of the Chateau

A flourishing economy and artistic life failed to cushion Nice from an ominous political situation. Once again Savoy, France and Spain were locked in a power struggle that erupted when French forces under Louis XIV occupied Savoy and Nice in 1691. Although the Treaty of Turin returned Nice to Savoy in 1697, peace was short-lived. The War of Spanish Succession broke out and Savoy broke its alliance with France who promptly attacked Nice again. The city capitulated at the end of 1705 and in 1706 French forces demolished the Chateau, reducing the walls, towers and bastions to rubble. Nice lost its military function and became part of France until it was returned to Savoy in 1748.

A New Start

As Nice was no longer a military outpost worth attacking, the city was free to concentrate on expansion and beautification. Grand public spaces such as the Cours Saleya and Place Garibaldi emerged, a new cemetery opened for burials on the Colline du Chateau, and the farmlands of west Nice finally got a parish church (Sainte Hélène). Construction began on the Port Lympia which was linked to Turin by a new road. Most importantly, the town became known to English aristocrats thanks to Scottish writer Tobias Smollett who wrote a bestseller about his experience in mid-18th century Nice. The first winter tourists began arriving, sparking Nice's eventual identity as a tourist destination.

The Revolution

When the French Revolution broke out in 1789, Savoy was left flatfooted. The duchy had little sympathy with revolutionary sentiments and allied with Austria to repel the Revolutionary army marching through Europe. Nice and the surrounding region were occupied and annexed to France following a "vote" that was neither free nor fair.

The period following the annexation was tumultuous with various factions fighting for or against the French, mostly in the hinterlands. The anti-clericalism of the Revolutionary regime was highly unpopular in Nice which saw its old religious orders—Franciscans, Jesuits, Dominicans, Carmelites, Minims—driven out. Also unpopular was the corruption of local officials which allowed men such as Andre Gastaud to buy up a vast chunk of land in west Nice. Abolishing Nice's status as a *port franc* dealt a blow to the local economy.

Bonaparte

Heroes also emerged during the post-Revolutionary period. When Napoleon Bonaparte launched his Italian campaign from Nice in 1796, he recruited a local officer, Andre Masséna, whose name is commemorated throughout town. Born in Nice in 1758 to a family of merchants, Masséna enlisted in the French army and quickly rose through the ranks despite his humble origins. He served with distinction in Bonaparte's Italian campaign and was made a Marshal of the Empire in 1804. The Emperor affectionately nicknamed him "the darling of victory".

Kingdom of Savoy-Sardinia

By the beginning of the 19th century, Nice soured on the empire along with the rest of France. When Napoleon abdicated in 1814 the Treaty of Paris returned Nice to Savoy, now known as the Kingdom of Savoy-Sardinia. It was a welcome change as "Frenchification" never caught on in Nice. Locals remained attached to their language, *Nissart*, and their many religious traditions despite an influx of French immigrants.

The kingdom lost no time in restoring Nice's sputtering economy and improving the infrastructure that had been allowed to languish. They modernized the city with public lighting and paved roads and turned the ruins of the old Chateau into a park. Nice's status as *port franc* was restored and the port was enlarged. Construction of the Pont Neuf over the Paillon river in 1824 allowed the town to expand westward.

Urbanization

The expansion project was vital because tourism was becoming an increasingly significant part of the local economy. The trickle of English visitors in the 18th century became a steady stream, growing throughout the 19th century. Other nationalities followed—French, Germans, Russians and Americans—lured by the mild winters and vistas of sun, sea and mountains. The English had already "colonized" the *Croix de Marbre* neighborhood across the river and called it Newborough. In 1824 they built the forerunner of the Promenade des Anglais, the *Chemin des Anglais*.

To manage an expanding and modernizing city, Savoy appointed an urban planning commission, the Consiglio d' Ornato, composed of prominent local merchants, nobles, jurists and architects. The commission proposed new roads, public spaces and infrastructure projects, regulated the style of buildings, the size of boulevards and the organization of streets. All building projects needed the commission's approval. Its primary focus were the neighborhoods popular with foreigners: the rue Saint François-de-Paule and nearby streets, the right quay of the Paillon river, the Promenade des Anglais and Newborough. Under its direction the Place Masséna, Jardin Albert 1er, and avenue Jean Médecin were laid out while Place Garibaldi and Port Lympia gained elegant new buildings. As Vieux Nice was considered poor and decrepit, that part of town was mostly left alone.

The urban improvements endeared the Niçois to their Savoy-Sardinian masters but the good feelings came to an abrupt halt when their overlords abolished Nice's status as a *port franc* in 1853. The great port of Genoa became the star of Piedmont, condemning Nice's little Port Lympia to irrelevance. It was a devastating blow to the local economy and led to violent demonstrations.

Vive la France

The port issue was also a key factor in Nice deciding to become a part of France in 1860. The Sardinian king needed the assistance of France to expel the Austrians who had invaded central Italy and impeded his project of Italian unification. France was willing to help because a unified Italy provided a counterweight to powerful Austria.

All was settled by the treaty of Turin in 1860 in which France aided Savoy-Sardinia in their struggle against Austria in exchange for Nice and Savoy. The rulers set up a referendum to validate the decision. Although the local population was initially divided, bitterness about the port coupled with pressure from the pro-France clergy, civil service and economic elites carried the day. The vote was 25,743 for and 160 against unification. And so ended five centuries of Savoy influence.

Fun City

Unification accelerated Nice's development as a tourist destination. With the opening of the train station in 1864, the Paris-Nice train disgorged a parade of wealthy or titled visitors. They poured into richly decorated hotels along the Promenade des Anglais and Cimiez or built elaborate mansions in the new Quartier des Musiciens neighborhood. Some created vast estates in west Nice. Belle Epoque style was in vogue and architects vied to construct the most ornate, opulent structures the owners could afford. Nice became the European capital of fun and entertainment.

The party came to an end with the outbreak of WWI in 1914. As tourists fled and the grand hotels were turned into military hospitals, the local economy crumbled. 3665 Niçois gave their lives in WWI; their deaths were commemorated on the Monument Aux Morts.

After the war, British visitors returned but the now impecunious Russians were replaced by a new generation of Americans. Eschewing the old-fashioned Belle Epoque palaces in Cimiez, these young visitors flocked to the hotels along the Promenade des Anglais, attracted to the terrace bars, casinos and swimming pools. Sea-bathing came into fashion and Nice became a summer destination. There were regattas in the Baie des Anges and auto races on the newly widened Promenade des Anglais. Jazz musicians such as Louis Armstrong came to play and artists such as Matisse and Raoul Dufy came to paint. Unlike 19th century visitors, no one came for their "health". They came to party.

The Art Deco Years

The interwar period also saw the emergence of a new style of architecture: Art Deco. Gone were the cherub-infested friezes that characterized Belle Epoque buildings. Instead, architects opted for clean, geometric lines and buildings decorated with mosaics, ceramics and paintings inspired by nature. They experimented with a variety of materials: reinforced concrete, stone and brick, sometimes all in the same structure. Right angles were banished in favor of rounded corners. Bow windows add visual interest to the facades and ironwork patterns enliven doors, railings and balconies. The apogee of Art Deco style is the Palais de la Méditerranée on the Promenade des Anglais but the style is most prevalent in the Quartier des Musiciens.

Occupation

WWII was a time of tremendous hardship in Nice. The Italian occupation (1940-1943) raised fears that Nice would once again become part of Italy. Resistors engaged in sabotage were duly jailed and tortured by Italian authorities based in Cimiez. The Italians were unenthused about deporting the Jewish population so many French Jews flocked to Nice as a safe haven.

The German occupation that lasted from December 1943 to August 1944 was far harsher. Over 3000 Jews were either deported or shot on the spot under German occupation. The Germans militarized the Colline du Chateau and used it to bombard the Old Town in the final days of the war. Throughout both occupations hunger, if not outright famine, was widespread throughout Nice as food supplies were disrupted.

The Modern Age

After the war Nice rebuilt and then built and built to accommodate a growing population. New apartment buildings replaced the old villas in Cimiez. Sprawling estates in west Nice were torn down in favor of public parks and posh residences. Decrepit neighborhoods in Vieux Nice were razed and rebuilt in traditional style. A new airport arose in response to the demands of mass tourism.

Nice's modernization continued in the 21st century with the construction of two tramway lines to relieve gnarled traffic in the town center. New bike lanes constructed by Mayor Christian Estrosi crisscross the town, making bicycles a pleasant mode of transport and recreation. The Promenade du Paillon or Coulée Verte turned the covered Paillon river into an oasis of greenery.

Ambitious new projects centered around the airport and train station are in development with the aim of attracting business travelers. Surely the century will see even more changes in this ancient yet always modern city.

OLD TOWN:
THE VIBRANT HEART

Start Opéra-Vieille Ville tram stop

Finish Tour Saint-François

Time 3 hours

Good for Art, architecture, historic monuments, churches

Points of Interest Palais Lascaris, Cours Saleya, Cathedral, L'Eglise de l'Annonciation, Jewish Quarter, Eglise du Gesù

Points to Note Palais Lascaris is closed Tuesday; many churches are only open for visits Tuesday afternoons

With its narrow, shady streets, cozy squares, colorful markets, baroque churches and jumble of pastel houses, the Old Town looks and feels much as it must have about two centuries ago. It was around then when the Old Town (or Vieux Nice or Vieille Ville) became known as "Le Babazouk" from an Algerian merchant who thought the neighborhood resembled his beloved Bazoum quarter in Algiers.

The sounds are different now, at least at night when music from the bars and nightclubs fills the air with rhythm. Young clubbers prowling the streets for the latest hangout make the Old Town seem like a vast open-air party. But during the day the streets are bustling with people on their way to work or the market, ready to shop or dine, greet friends or gossip in a cafe in Nice's most convivial and least pretentious neighborhood.

HISTORY

The story of Vieux Nice began when people drifted down from the Colline du Chateau to settle around the Franciscan monastery in the late 13th century. The eastern part of Old Nice closest to Castle Hill was settled first. Naturally these settlers needed protection so the walls of Castle Hill were extended to circle their territory. The 14th-century Pairolière tower near the church of Saint Augustin formed a corner of the fortifications surrounding the town. (The remains of the Pairolière tower and the ancient walls can be visited on a tour of Nice's Archaeological Crypt).

With the *ville haute* on top of the hill as an administrative and military center, the *ville basse* below developed into a commercial center importing wheat from Lombardy and salt from Toulon and Hyères. A 14th century succession struggle left Nice in the hands of the House of Savoy, then based in Chambéry. The town became important both as an outlet to the sea and as a fortress-town.

Once the Turks and Franks besieged the Chateau in 1543, the *ville haute* was turned into a citadel and the civilian population moved down to Vieux Nice. The town thrived within an expanded fortification system. The old Cathedral on the hill was abandoned and a new one, dedicated to Saint Réparate, was built. Other churches and chapels followed.

Four of the most spectacular chapels were established by the Penitents brotherhoods. These Catholic brotherhoods originated in 13th-century Italy and appeared in Nice in the 14th century. Arising at a time when the idea of a "social safety net" was non-existent, the brotherhoods devoted themselves to caring for the poor, the elderly, the sick, orphans, widows and criminals condemned to death. The four Penitent brotherhoods in Nice are white, black, blue and red derived from the color of their robes and headdresses. The brotherhoods are still active and stage processions on religious holidays.

The Old Town developed first in the east which is where you'll find the oldest neighborhood with buildings dating from the 16th century. The center developed primarily in the 17th and 18th centuries which was the great age of baroque architecture. Towards the end of the 18th century the western part of town developed as a stylish district with fine housing and expensive shops.

During the 19th century other neighborhoods developed, primarily to lodge the many guests from northern Europe who came to Nice for their health. The new railway station made Nice an easy town to visit. After Nice voted to become part of France in 1860, wealthy families began building palatial residences in the newly chic neighborhoods of

Cimiez and the Quartier des Musiciens. Living in the Old Town lost its cachet.

From the middle of the 19th to the middle of the 20th century Vieux Nice was increasingly filthy and unhygienic. Many buildings didn't have heat, running water or electricity. Instead of sewage disposal people dumped their waste in the street or collected it in pots to be sold as fertilizer for nearby farms. Because few buildings had kitchens people ate their *socca*, grilled sardines and soup on the street. It became a neighborhood for poor people, many from France's former colonies in North Africa. As soon as anyone had the means to do so, they moved out.

In the 1950s and 1960s under mayor Jacques Médecin the most dilapidated buildings were torn down. Fortunately, the new constructions were designed with an eye to preserving the architectural look of the traditional buildings. Other buildings were structurally reinforced and their facades rejuvenated. Also in the 1960s a new emphasis on preserving France's heritage freed up funds for local rehabilitation projects.

Once the Old Town was presentable, artists and small boutiques moved in. Tourists soon followed and then the bars and restaurants that catered to them. The boom in vacation rentals encouraged people to buy apartments, rehabilitate them and rent them. Even though the sound of wheeled suitcases clattering down the streets is new for the locals, most have adapted well. And why not? Old Nice has withstood the ravages of time for 700 years without losing its soul and is ready to take on the next millennium.

NOTE that the streets of Vieux Nice have two names on the street signs. Above is the current name in French and below is the original name, not a translation, in *Nissart*, Nice's local dialect. Although no longer spoken *Nissart* is derived from the Occitan language.

528

VIEUX NICE. — La Rue Providence, Place Sainte-Claire

Collections ND Phot

Start at the Opéra-Vieille Ville tram stop on the boulevard Jean Jaurès. You're standing on top of the ramparts that once served to protect Vieux Nice from the Paillon river that was covered over in 1868.

Paillon River 1865

Go down the steps and take the first right onto rue Raoul Bosio. On the right at No 3 is the

(1) Palais Corvésy, an example of the majestic
palaces erected by Nice nobility in the 18th century. It was Clément Corvesy, Count of Gorbio, who built the palace in 1769. Perhaps it's fairer to say that the palace is a reproduction of an 18th-century palace as the original building has been overhauled several times since its construction. The facade was painted with trompe l'oeil techniques to resemble the original baroque style. Now used as an official building (*Mairie Annexe*), it's usually not a problem to enter during business hours to look around. Pass through the monumental entranceway (and a metal detector) to admire the vast vestibule. Three vaulted bays create a light, airy look and the marble staircase with vaulted ceilings is one of the most beautiful in Nice.

Across the street take the passage, Espace Joseph Marro. The building on your left is the side of the

(2) Palais Rusca, built in 1776 as barracks for a city

garrison that could hold up to 725 men. It continued to be used as a barracks until 1990 when it became an annex of the Palais de Justice courts. Continue to the front entrance on the

(3) Place du Palais de Justice, the

demarcation point between not-so-old Nice to the west and very old Nice to the east. Until 1705 when Louis XIV blew up the town walls, this square was the western limits of Nice. It was named the Place Saint Dominique after the Dominican convent that dominated the square. Built in the 13th century and abandoned during the Revolution, the convent was finally destroyed in 1887.

With the wall gone, a lot of space opened up for development. The area between here and the mouth of the Paillon river to the east was an undeveloped marshland, the *Prè-aux-Oies* (Geese Meadow). Developers lost no time in laying out new streets and palaces, an urbanization that accelerated in 1868 when the Paillon river was covered over and access became easier. From 1776 when the Palais Rusca barracks was built, the whole square was the scene of daily military exercises. Finally in 1823, the neighbors had enough and demanded that military training be moved elsewhere.

Looming over the square is the 19th-century **Palais de Justice** (Courthouse) which replaced the former Dominican convent. The colossal neoclassical structure seems like "the majesty of the law" expressed in stone. Inaugurated in 1892, the building is the work of local architect Auguste-Vincent Diedé-Défly (1845-1903).

Place Saint Dominique with Dominican convent on the right

You can't miss the **Clock Tower** which dates from 1718. A plaque on the bottom is a reminder that it was erected during the reign of Victor-Amédée II, oddly referred to as the *Roi de Sicile* (King of Sicily), a title he only held for seven years. Plaques also commemorate the deaths of two WWII Resistance fighters on August 28, 1944, the date of the liberation of Nice. Both were born in Italy and were killed by mortar shells fired from the Colline du Chateau as Germans made their last stand.

Every Saturday the square hosts an open-air **book market** (7am-5pm) with stands full of first editions, old books, postcards and more.

At the northern edge of the square with a highly ornate wrought-iron entrance is the

(4) Palais des Spitalieri de Cessole at No 5 rue
de la Préfecture. The powerful Spitalieri family built this palace from 1762 to 1768 and it soon became the home of the French Consulate (remember that Nice was part of Savoy at the time). When Thomas Jefferson was America's ambassador to France he spent three days here in 1787. Nice

was a particular pleasure for Jefferson as he was a big fan of Nice's famous Bellet wines.

When Nice became a fashionable winter destination in the early 19th century, the palace became the Hotel d'York and welcomed notables such as Giuseppe Garibaldi as well as all the popular musicians and performers of the day. It was one of the first hotels in Nice. The building is usually locked but if not you'll see a well-restored entrance hall of marble and slate with vaulted ceilings and marble stairs.

Follow rue de la Préfecture a few steps to the east and you'll come to No 6, the

(5) Spaggiari Window. True-crime fans may recall the saga of Albert Spaggiari whose team tunneled under the Societé Generale bank in 1976, to commit the "heist of the century". Entering the bank vaults through sewers, Spaggiari and his cohorts seized some 30-100 million francs, leaving a note that read *sans armes, ni haine, ni violence* ("without weapons, hatred, or violence"). He was arrested in 1977 and brought to a judge's office here for questioning. While the judge was distracted trying to decipher a document that Spaggiari forged, the enterprising crook jumped out the first floor window and onto a waiting motorcycle. The window through which he escaped is the one on the right over the wooden entrance door.

Well, dear reader, he got away with it. His entanglements with local politicians and even international spies caused an eruption of accusations and finger-pointing but the money was never found and Spaggiari spent the rest of his life in Argentina and Italy. He died in 1989.

Return to the Place du Palais and head south across the square. On the right is the

(6) Cafe du Palais which occupies the bottom floor

of the **Palais Torrini de Fougassières**. Built in 1750 for an aristocratic Nice family, this palace was the first to be constructed after the destruction of the town walls. Peek inside to look at the marvelous stucco and frescoes. The cafe is a highly popular spot to linger over coffee and people-watch.

Make a right on rue Alexandre Mari and at No 15 is the sober facade of the

(7) Palais Héraud, another home for the rich and

powerful. Built in 1757, the palace passed from the Héraud family to the Lascaris, Malausséna and Raiberti families. The austere exterior contrasts with a unique spiral staircase inside, all curves and columns.

Continue to rue Raoul Bosio. On the corner, notice the small **medallion** on the wall. It's of Saint François de Paule. Vieux Nice was divided into official neighborhoods called *insulae* in Latin or *ilots* (islands) in French. They were named after saints and often included their likeness as a reminder. Make a left. At No 7 rue Raoul Bosio is the

(8) Cave Bianchi, a cheerful wine cellar that dates

back to 1860. It was once the cellars of the Dominican monastery and remains an excellent address for wine-lovers.

Continue to rue Saint-François de Paule. Right in front of you is the

(9) Opéra de Nice, 4-6 rue Saint-François-de-Paule. The billboards announcing coming events is a sure-fire sign that you're in the right place. The Nice opera house is still central to Nice's cultural life as home to the Nice Philharmonic, the Nice Opera and the Nice Ballet.

The opera house was a favorite of 19th-century composers. Jules Massenet debuted his work *Marie-Madeleine* here. Giacomo Puccini personally directed rehearsals for *Manon Lescaut* here in 1893.

The first opera house on this spot dates from 1826 but it was not destined to last. On March 23, 1881 no sooner had the curtain risen on a production of *Lucia di Lamermoor* than the building was engulfed in flames. A gas leak provoked the blaze that left 63 people dead immediately but the ultimate toll is thought to have reached 200. Those in the orchestra and loges were able to escape but those in the cheaper seats on top were trapped. A monument to the dead was placed in the cemetery of the Colline du Chateau.

Rebuilding was contemplated immediately but ran into opposition. Some said that Vieux Nice was passé and that the Opera should be in a trendier neighborhood. Traditionalists won and local architect François Aune took over the project. The new building was inaugurated in 1885 with a production of Verdi's *Aida*.

The overall neoclassical style was retained for the facade which combines Piedmontese and French influences. The majestic rotunda on the east side links the north and east facades with columns and large windows that are illuminated on opera nights. Notice the statues of the four Muses on the pillars of the upper terrace: Euterpe (Music), Melpomene (Tragedy), Thalia (Comedy), Terpsichore (Dance).

Most of the materials used were local. Stones were from La Turbie; sand came from the Var or Magnan; pebbles used in the concrete foundation came from Contes. The southern side facing the sea is much more austere.

Enter the vestibule during box office hours for a glimpse of the grand staircase and balustrade that leads to the orchestra. The orchestra is a lush affair with loges, gilt and red tapestry and an impressive ceiling fresco. Apollo's son Phaeton drives the chariot of the Sun in what could be an allusion to mastering the fire that destroyed the prior building. Other mythological scenes show Apollo and Aphrodite surrounded by various creatures from Greek myths.

The Nice Opera runs tours of the interior by reservation. The season runs from September to June. Orchestra seats can sell out quickly mainly because it's the only part of the opera house that offers comfortable seating. See the website: opera-nice.org.

Across the street from the opera is the

(10) L'Eglise Saint-François-de-Paule, built

as part of the 18th-century urbanization of the *Prè-aux-Oies*. The name comes from Saint-François de Paule who established the Order of Minims. This mendicant order, now disappeared, came to Nice in 1633 and began building the church in 1722 on what was then the most stylish street in town. Their motto, "Charitas", appears on a medallion over the entrance. The Dominican Order acquired the church in 1934 and has retained it ever since.

The sober, gray exterior is styled after buildings in Turin which was the capital of the House of Savoy, Nice's governors. The interior displays an exuberant assortment of sculptures, medallions and paintings. Particularly noteworthy is *La Communion de Saint Benoit* by Jean-Baptiste Van Loo in the first chapel on the right. The church is now a popular place for classical music concerts.

While on rue Saint-François de Paule, take a look at some of the classic shops that have been there for generations. There's **Maison Auer** (No 7) that has been making sweets, candied fruit and chocolates here since 1820. Pop inside for a riot of Belle Epoque style. **La Cougeto** (No 8) has been selling Provençal fabrics and santons since 1947. **Alziari** (No 14) is known for its fresh, local olive oil. Founded in 1878, the company still uses a traditional olive mill made out of white stone from La Turbie.

Across from Alziari at No 5 rue Hotel de Ville is the stately

(11) Hotel de Ville or Town Hall which has undergone a lot of permutations over the centuries. The building began as a seminary in 1750 but was requisitioned by the army of the King of Sardinia to install troops there in 1791. It was transformed into a prison in 1793, then a gendarmerie, a hospital and a gendarmerie again before becoming a town hall in 1868. Most of what you see dates from 1866 when the facade was redesigned. Another redesign with an Art Deco interior took place in 1928.

Retrace your steps and next to the opera at No 2 is the

(12) Palais Hongran. Behind the sober facade lies one of the Old Town's most splendid interiors. Built between 1769 and 1772, this private residence welcomed Napoleon for a week in 1796. He stayed on the top floor. Bonaparte arrived just after he married Josephine and was named head of the Army of Italy. It was a crucial moment for the young general. The Army of Italy was in terrible shape, ragged, demoralized and starving when Bonaparte arrived here on March 26. On March 27 he delivered his famous proclamation: "You are naked, malnourished; the government owes you a lot. . . Your patience, the courage that you show in the midst of these rocks, are admirable; but it does not bring you any glory. . . I want to lead you to the most fertile plains in the world. Rich provinces, big cities will be in your power; you will find honor, glory and riches there". It was enough to rally the soldiers who went on to secure him the victory that made his illustrious career.

The building became the first municipal library in 1838 and then a museum. The Shah of Iran stayed here about a century ago obviously attracted by the sumptuous decor.

The first thing that grabs the eye is the monumental 18th-century staircase and four cores with stacked columns. Even more eye-popping are the Art Nouveau frescoes that enliven the walls and ceilings. Painted by Maurice Pillard-Verneuil (1869-1942), there are few examples of this style in Nice.

The building is a historic monument, used for vacation rentals (palais-hongran.com), and is locked. You can glimpse the interior through the grate but it's worth entering if the door is open.

Now you're at the edge of

(13) Cours Saleya, the sensual center of life in the Old Town. The daily morning market is thronged with food and flower shoppers from Tuesday to Sunday. No sooner do the shoppers clear out than the restaurants set up their outdoor tables for lunch. On Monday mornings the piles of fresh fruit and vegetables yield to stalls selling antiques and bric-a-brac.

Old Nice's sunniest spot has undergone a series of changes over the centuries. Until the 13th century what is now Cours Saleya was an extension of the port Saint Lambert. Roughly corresponding to the area now occupied by Castel Plage, Saint Lambert was Nice's only commercial port. Later the Saint Lambert port became known as the Ponchettes. Fishermen brought back their catch and larger boats deposited salt from the salt beds of Hyéres west of Nice. There was a large fish market and a number of warehouses to store the salt.

In 1250 the first ramparts were built, running along the sea in what is now rue Barillerie, just north of the Cours Saleya. When Duke Emmanuel Philibert built his palace here (now the Palais de la Prefecture, below) in the mid-16th-century, other public buildings. sprang up in the vicinity. They needed protection so in 1575 the walls were moved to the south along the sea. Meanwhile, most of the current Cours Saleya was the Duke's private garden.

By the beginning of the 18th century, the Turkish threat had receded and the ramparts were transformed into stores and warehouses for the fishing business as well as little houses for fishermen. In 1776, the tops of the buildings were turned into garden-promenade for the *Niçois* elite to take a healthy stroll along the sea. Known as the *Terrasses* or *Terrasses des Ponchettes,* the garden-promenade was enlarged and expanded over the following centuries. Now it's just known as the Ponchettes.

In 1861 the mayor, Malausséna, observed that the markets of Saint-François and Rossetti were running out of space. He decided that Cours Saleya had plenty of space and so decreed that the flower market would occupy the west side of the Cours, and produce on the east side, an arrangement that continues today.

In the 20th century the markets and warehouses became art galleries. A group of renowned artists that included Matisse and Pierre Bonnard threw their weight behind a project intending to showcase contemporary Mediterranean art. The galleries—Ponchettes and Marine—attracted the most famous artists of the day including Bonnard and Matisse, Marc Chagall, Jean Cocteau and Raoul Dufy. Unfortunately, the galleries have recently been demolished as part of a plan to create open spaces between the Cours Saleya and the sea.

Where does the unusual name, Saleya, come from anyway? There are a number of theories but no one knows for sure. Maybe the old *Nissart* word *Soleiya* which means "sunny"? Or maybe from the word *salins* which refers to the salt that was the center of the region's commerce? I prefer the first because the Cours Saleya is indeed sunny.

Go up the left side of the Cours to admire the beautifully restored late 18th century baroque buildings. Then on your left you'll see the

(14) Palais de la Préfecture also known as the
Palais des Rois de Sardaigne. If the building looks fit for a king, well that's the idea. At the time of its original construction in the 16th century, Savoy Duke Emmanuel Philibert, ruled Nice. The Duke had spent most of his adolescence in Nice and when he achieved power in 1553 he decided to build a residence here. His reasons were not purely sentimental. At that time Nice was considered an important provincial capital. Sadly his original construction was destroyed in a fire in 1610. Reconstruction began immediately and the new building was inaugurated in 1614.

As befitting such a stately structure, the Palais lodged local officials throughout the 17th century and received a succession of European nobility on state visits to Nice. In the early 18th century the House of Savoy acquired Sardinia and the ducal house became a royal house. When France annexed Nice in 1792 and the revolutionary army swept through, the building became a military hospital.

When the Treaty of Paris restored Nice to Savoy-Sardinian rule, the royal palace became a royal palace again. A massive overhaul restored its former glory in 19th century style both inside and outside. Kings Charles-Félix, Charles-Albert and Victor Emmanuel stayed here and when Nice became a part of France in 1860 Napoleon III and his wife made a visit. Throughout the 19th and 20th century the Palais expanded in both size and richness of decor. It was here that the Treaty of Nice, defining the EU's legislative powers, was signed in 2001.

Can you imagine a flag with a swastika draped over such an illustrious building? Neither could astonished Cours Saleya shoppers one morning in September 2015. As a man unfurled the Nazi flag and hung it on the building people began shouting. Some cried. It seemed that the trauma of WWII was very much alive. When cameras rolled up, people discovered that it was all part of a movie set. The building was used for a scene in *Un Sac des Billes* (A Bag of Marbles), a film about occupied France.

Currently the Palais de la Préfecture is the residence of the Prefect of Nice and is only open to the public each September on the annual *Journées du Patrimoine*

What is open to the public is the

(15) Musée de la Photographie also to your left at 1 Place Pierre Gautier. It's fun to duck in to check out the collection of old and new images from a variety of regional photographers. *(closed Monday)*

Cross to the other side of the market and take the stairs to the top of the "Terrasses" at the **Porte Royale** where the Dukes entered their palace. This is where fashionable folks took a stroll in the 18th and 19th centuries. Although the rooftop promenade is now closed, it's a great view over the Cours Saleya. On the other side is a **statue of former President Jacques Chirac** by Nice artist Patrick Frega. Inaugurated in 2020, the statue was controversial as the former President was convicted on corruption-related charges before his death.

Just beyond the Palace on the north side of the Cours Saleya is the stunning

(16) Chapelle de la Miséricorde a magnificent

testament to the prestige of the Cours Saleya. Built in 1740, it's considered a masterpiece of baroque architecture and has been named a historic monument. The interior is a dazzling display of frescoes and gilt yet the relatively small size gives it an aura of intimacy.

The story of the chapel begins with the Order of Theatines who built a convent here in 1671. In the early 18th century they acquired more land and decided to expand. They hired Bernardo Vittone, a favored architect in Savoy, to somehow combine the convent and a new chapel. In an ingenious sleight of hand, he managed to make it look as though the convent and chapel are a single building. Look closely at the front to see that the monks' cells are above the central oculus (circular window). On the side, the oculi also separate the chapel from the living quarters but here the windows are angled to let light into the nave.

The Theatines were chased out during the Revolution soon after the interior decor was finished in 1786. The building then became a warehouse, library and theater before the Black Penitents bought it in 1828.

The Penitents immediately embarked upon a lavish restoration project but kept the original oval floor plan of the Saint Gaëtan chapel. Notice the cycle of paintings from the 18th and 19th centuries that depict the Virgin, various patrons of the brotherhood as well as notables from the Theatines. On the high altar Nice painter Hercule Trachel (1820-1872) created the four cardinal virtues. The Virgin is also depicted in the *Vierge de Misèricorde* (1429) by Montpelier artist Jean Mirailhet and again by artist Louis Bréa (1515).
(open for religious services and Tuesday afternoon)

In front of the Miséricorde Chapel is the famous **Chez Theresa**, a simple socca stall that has become Nice's most famous culinary institution. Sometime the last century, a certain Theresa, of Italian origin, brought her mobile oven to the Cours Saleya and introduced Nice to *socca*. Made from chick pea flour, water, olive oil and salt, the mixture is poured onto a round, flat plate and cooked at high heat. The result is a flat, thin pancake that is cut up into triangles, sprinkled with black pepper and eaten warm. Although there have been three "Theresas", the tradition continues every market day (Tuesday-Sunday mornings). Also on sale are other Nice specialties such as *pissaladière* (onion pie), *tourte de blette* (swiss chard tart), and *pan bagnat* (tuna, egg and vegetable sandwich).

Next to the Chapel is the

(17) Palais Grimaldi, a handsome building built at

the turn of the 17th century. Unfortunately, Count Grimaldi (yes, from the same Grimaldi family that founded Monaco) was arrested for treason and executed soon after the construction.

At the eastern end of the Cours Saleya is a majestic old building, the

(18) Palais Caïs de Pierlas where Matisse lived

and worked from 1921 to 1938. He rented an apartment on the third floor overlooking Cours Saleya and then moved up to a nine-room apartment on the fourth floor where he had a view of the market and the sea. Here he painted the *Odalisque Tatouée*, *La Robe Tilleul*, and the *Grand Nu Couché*.

Why Nice? The artist explains: "Nice ... why Nice? In my art I tried to create a crystalline environment for the mind: this necessary clarity, I found in Nice. In reality it's admirable. Everything becomes clear, crystalline, precise, limpid."

The Palais Caïs Pierlas is also one of the oldest buildings in Nice. Built in 1693 for the Ribotti family, the building was used as a school from 1729 when the Jesuit college was closed. The stuccoes over the 2nd floor represent the four liberal arts: grammar, drawing, architecture and music. The Caïs de Pierlas family bought the building in 1782.

The arched double doorway leading to the Promenade des Anglais is the **Porte Charles-Félix** opened in 1826 to welcome King Charles-Félix on his visit to Nice in 1826.

Next to the Palais is the

(19) Chapelle du Saint-Suaire et de la Très Sainte-Trinité a Red Penitents chapel. The unusual name refers to the fusion of three brotherhoods. First there was the brotherhood of the Saint Nom de Jésus which was founded in 1578. Then came the brotherhood of Saint Esprit founded in 1585. The brotherhood of Saint Suaire was founded in 1620 and named after the Holy Shroud (*Saint Suaire*) which was held in Nice's Colline du Chateau from 1536 to 1543. They built a chapel here in 1657.

The brotherhood of Saint Nom de Jésus merged with the brotherhood of Saint Esprit in 1782. The original chapel was ravaged during the Revolution. After the Revolution the brotherhood of Saint Esprit fused with the brotherhood of Saint Suaire. In 1824 the chapel was entrusted to the Red Penitents who merged all the brotherhoods under the name of Most Holy Trinity.

By the time the new brotherhood was ready to rebuild their chapel in 1824, the baroque style was giving way to Neo-classicism, a more austere style. Over the entrance is a semi-circle with the Triangle of the Trinity. The small bell tower is covered in tiles in Genoese style.

Inside is a splendid altar crowned with the *La Sainte-Trinité* .painting by Emile Barberi (1775-1847). Even more impressive are paintings from the original 17th-century chapel: *Mise au Tombeau* and *l'Ostension du Saint-Suaire* by Nice artist Jean-Gaspard Baldoino (1590-1669) which respectively depict the burial and display of the Holy Shroud.

In the organ gallery, a door communicated with the neighboring Senate. Before the annual start of the judicial session, the senators attended a special mass which was intended to help them render justice.

(open Tuesday 10am-noon, 2-5pm)

Next door to the church at No 14 rue Jules Gilly duck into the

(20) Nice Sénat, Nice's old Senate building, now the

Centre du Patrimoine (Heritage Center). It's a good place to pick up maps and leaflets about Nice and also to revisit a bit of Nice's history.

Nice's Senate was created by the Duke of Savoy, Charles-Emmanuel in 1614. The name implies some degree of popular rule but no. The Senate was composed of ambitious lawyers and essentially served as a courthouse and tribunal where all political and administrative matters were settled. Judges tended to commercial regulations, royal edicts, border issues, the organization of religious groups, prison management, the rights and privileges of the local nobility, building churches and more. The three-story building had various halls that were elaborately decked out with tapestries, paintings and furniture.

When Nice voted to become part of France in 1860, judicial reorganization and the needs of a growing community prompted the construction of the new Palais de Justice and everything eventually moved there. The Senate fell into disrepair and was used for various civic purposes, including an association for the blind and lodging for convalescing mothers, until its renovation in 2012. As part of archaeological research, part of Nice's original **medieval wall**, standing from the 13th to 17th centuries, was discovered and is visible inside.

Peek around the corner at rue de l'Ancien Sénat and to see the **loggia** where announcements were posted and people could discuss their grievances with a government representative. It eventually became an *accueil de nuit* where indigent people could sleep or take a shower. Up until the mid-20th century it was used as a public bath house since there were still people in Vieux Nice without running water. The sign "Dovches" is the Latinized *Douches* or Showers.

The entire length of the rue de l'Ancien Sénat housed prison cells. Go up a few steps to No 2 and you're in front of the **executioner's house**. The job of "executioner" was passed from father to son until 1860. When Nice became French there was no longer a town executioner. Instead, an executioner with a portable guillotine would arrive by train from Paris. The death penalty was abolished in France in 1981.

Return to the Senate and right across the street is a

(21) Lintel at No 7 where "1721" is inscribed over an ironwork transom. Lintels with inscriptions are a regular feature in this, the oldest part of Vieux Nice. Most have religious symbols which, it was believed, placed the house under divine protection. There are all varieties of crosses. Every so often there's a play on words, a reference to the house's owner, the date of its construction, a proverb, a coat-of-arms. There are 61 lintels in Vieux Nice.

Another feature of this part of Vieux Nice is the ironwork transom or *clairoir* above the lintel. These open transoms serve an important practical function: they keep the interior cool. Originally there was a vestibule behind the door that ran vertically to the top of the building which was partially covered with glass. The difference between the streets cooled by night air and the heat under the roof created an air current that ventilated the building. The narrow, shuttered windows also helped this natural air-conditioning system. Now that elevators have been installed in many of the vestibules the natural cooling has stopped and many of the apartments have air-conditioners.

Make a left on rue Barillerie. Note that this street was originally the site of the 13th century walls. On the corner of rue de la Poissonnerie over a spice shop is the

(22) "Adam and Eve" fresco depicting a nearly nude and obviously perturbed couple in a garden. Sculpted in 1584 using an Italian technique known as *sgraffito,* the battling couple seems to be far from the Garden of Eden. Some say that the fresco was inspired by the quarreling couples that inhabited the premises at the time. Others say it depicts a long-forgotten local festival, *Festin des reproches* where couples were encouraged to playfully enact their conflicts in public.

Turn right on rue de la Poissonnerie and at No 2 is the

(23) Palais de Pons Ceva, dating from the late 17th century. Behind the late baroque entrance is an elegant vestibule with curved Tuscan columns, moldings and a harmonious staircase with wrought-iron balustrades. It's all beautifully restored and softly lit.

Across the street is the delightful

(24) L'Eglise de l'Annonciation, popularly known as **Sainte Rita**, Vieux Nice's most beloved and delightfully intimate churches. Walking into the sparkling interior is like finding yourself inside a jewelry box.

Saint Rita is the patron saint of lost and impossible causes. The main lost cause that Rita was battling was an abusive husband to whom she was pressed into marriage at the age of 12. When he was finally murdered in a vendetta, she dissuaded her sons from exacting revenge. Saintly! She entered a convent and displayed a stigmata in 1442 that lasted until her death in 1457.

It was the Benedictine order that first established a chapel here around the 10th century, making Saint Rita the oldest religious site in Nice. It became a parish in 1493 and in 1604 the Carmelites took over. They extended the chapel and built a friary around it. After finding the church "narrow, inconvenient and dark" they decided to expand it to an adjoining building and undertake a total renovation. It was completed by the end of the 17th century at the height of the baroque period. The bell tower topped with a Rococo dome was built in 1740.

The Carmelites were chased out in a fit of Revolutionary fervor in 1793 and the church became a salt warehouse. By 1806 it was just a simple chapel.

After a fire in 1834 ravaged the old building, the church was renovated and a new facade created. As the original altar painting went up in smoke, the Russian painter Chevelkine contributed *L'Annonciation* to the apse and the church acquired that name. The church was entrusted to the Oblate order who are still in charge.

In 1934, Father Andrea Bianco, then rector of the church, installed a statue of Saint Rita in the first side altar after the entrance. She was an immediate hit among the locals especially during the dark years of WWII when normal life seemed like a lost cause. The church was classified a historic monument in 1947.

The interior has a simple floor plan but the baroque styling gives an impression of incredible richness. The first chapel on the right is to **Saint Erasmus** who was the patron saint of sailors. In the central painting Saint Erasmus extends his hand to save a sinking ship while the lower cartouche of the altar depicts various navigation instruments.

Next is the **Chapel of the Immaculate Heart of Mary** which depicts a diverse collection of saints whose connection is mysterious. Above the painting is a heart of carved wood, pierced with a dagger, which can be opened and which contains the list of the members of the founding brotherhood. On the left is a portrait of the hermit Saint Anthony who was the patron saint of the porters association in Nice. Their symbol was a pig which is visible to the right of the painting. Nothing derogatory there. The porters were authorized to have a pig, the only one allowed to wander the streets of Nice.

The artistic highlight is the **Chapel of the Madonna of Mount Carmel** with the white marble statue of the Virgin and Child carved around 1771 by the Genoese sculptor, Giovanni Andrea Ansaldo. The Madonna of Carmel protects the Carmelites who founded the church.

Saint Rita's chapel, adorned with flowers and votive candles, is just left of the entrance. The statue of Rita is a naïve work from the beginning of the 20th century. The chapel also contains a painting of the Madonna on the right wall who was the previous object of worship in this chapel. The left wall has a painting of Saint Elizabeth of Hungary.*(open daily, closed for lunch)*

Around the corner on rue de la Préfecture is the

(25) Loggia.

When the Carmelites took over the property, their original idea was to build a friary in the adjoining building. The problem was that the city had just built a loggia next to the church and had no interest in tearing it down. It was where all municipal decrees and edicts were handed down. It's still there adjoining the church and now displays medieval lintels and remnants of a column topped by a sphinx. The column and sphinx was a gift from the Jewish community to King Charles-Félix to celebrate his visit to Nice in 1826.

Continue a few steps more on rue de la Préfecture to the

(26) Stone house

at No 18 which may be the oldest intact buildings in Vieux Nice. The sealed Gothic arch on the side and the elegant Gothic windows above indicate that the building may have been constructed as far back as the 14th or 15th centuries. The exact date and purpose of the building is unknown but it may have been linked to the Church of the Annunciation (Saint Rita) when it was in the hands of the Benedictines. Another curious feature is the lack of a staircase in the four-story building. Access to the upper floors is via a staircase in the adjoining building. Now belonging to the furniture store **Fuscielli**, it's easy to enter and ask the owner's permission to tour the ancient vaulted basement.

Now turn around and head in the other direction on rue de la Prefecture. The street becomes **rue du Malonat,** one of the oldest roads in Vieux Nice. It provided an important link between the settlement at the top of the Colline du Chateau and the old port on Castel beach. Climb the stairs and check out the

(27) Lavoir (washtub) on the right, at the corner of rue de l'Ancien Sénat and rue du Malonat. It's the last public washtub left in Nice. Notice the niche for soap between the washing and rinsing sections. Laundry wasn't the only thing washed here. The washtub was conveniently located near the prison and executioner's house. After an execution the water ran red with blood as the executioners used the tub to wash their hatchets.

Next, notice the classical doorway at No 6 which was the entrance to the old

(28) Governor's Palace. This building was the source of one of Nice's most intriguing legends: **The Treasure of Malonat**. The story goes that one Bertrad d'Arlac, the daughter of the governor fell in love with one Auger Guigonis, a knight in the famous Knights Templar. This Catholic brotherhood had amassed fabulous wealth during the Crusades which raised the envy of France's King Philippe IV.

On 13 October 1307 the vengeful king rounded up every knight he could find and burned them at the stake. Auger Guigonis and some other Knights eluded capture and slipped away along with their treasure. The plan was to hide in Nice while organizing a getaway from the port of Antibes.

Bertrad and Auger met clandestinely here at her father's palace using elaborate passwords. One night, Bertrad told him of a conversation she had overheard in her father's presence indicating that the Knights were about to be arrested. Auger confided that he and the Knights were looking for a hideaway to stash their treasure.

Bertrad knew just the place. Rue Malonat was connected to secret subterranean tunnels in the nearby Colline du Chateau. She knew the network well and even had the keys. The following night Bertrad procured the old keys and guided a group of Knights laden with loot into the tunnels.

Her triumph was short-lived. Just days later Auger Guigonis and the other Knights were arrested, brought to Aix-en-Provence and burned at the stake. A distraught Bertrad threw herself from the top of the Chateau onto the rocks below. The vaunted treasure of the Knights Templar was never located underneath the Chateau but, then again, no one has ever looked for it.

Climb up rue du Malonat to see the

(29) Notre Dame du Malonat, a statue of the Virgin which was installed in 1854. At the time Nice was threatened by yet another cholera epidemic and the faithful needed a safe place to pray for deliverance. A special ceremony was organized August 2. The prayers worked.

Nice was spared the worst of the epidemic and the statue became the focus of a local cult. Each year since 1854 there are solemn processions and a special mass at the nearby Eglise du Gesù around the anniversary of the original ceremony.

Interest in the statue revived during WWII. The people gave thanks to the Virgin of Malonat for the "phony peace" of 1940. Then, there was widespread worry that the Italian occupiers would annex Nice. More prayers ensued which were successful. The arrival of the Germans in 1943 brought an Allied bombardment that resulted in 17 deaths when a building on rue Sainte Claire was hit. It could have been worse and locals were sure it would have been worse without the intervention of the Virgin.

Retrace your steps and turn right on rue Droite, one of the oldest streets in Nice. At the time "Droite" meant direct, not straight. The road was a direct link from the port in front of the Old Town through the town to the banks of the Paillon river. Later, it became known for its goldsmiths. In a few steps you'll arrive at the sprawling

(30) Palais des Galléan du Châteauneuf. The
Galléan family made their fortune in naval armaments and did so well that in the 17th century they erected a palace that takes up the entire block between the rue du Malonat and rue du Chateau. Divided up and sold after the French Revolution, it's now occupied by the **Acchiardo restaurant**. This highly popular restaurant dates back to 1927 and remains an excellent address to sample traditional Nice dishes. (Advance reservation highly recommended).

Take the rue Place Vieille in front of the restaurant to No 5 where there's a

(31) Lintel that reads Interna Meliora, translated as "Better Inside". What could it mean? A restaurant? Theater? No. It was a brothel! Continue on a few steps to the charming early 17th century **Place Vieille**, the oldest square in Nice.

Retrace your steps back to rue Droite, turn left and you'll quickly come to the

(32) Eglise Saint - Jacques - Le - Majeur,

popularly known as the **Eglise du Gesù,** a spectacular example of baroque architecture. There were two successive churches on this site, both built by the Jesuits. The first church, built in 1612, proved to be too small. Construction of the current church began in 1642 and finished in 1696.When the Jesuits were expelled in 1773, it became a parish church dedicated to Saint James the Great (*Saint Jacques Le Majeur*).

The original facade was unadorned but in 1825 it was recreated in fashionable baroque style. Notice the elegant Serlian window in the center covered with a semi-circular arch. On either side are niches with two allegorical figures: Hope with an anchor on the left and Faith with a cross on the right. The bell tower (visible from rue de la Croix) features exposed brick in Piedmontese style. The roof is shaped as a policeman's hat and covered with glazed tiles in Genoese style.

Eglise du Gesù was the first baroque church in Nice, vaguely modeled after the Church of the Gesù in Rome. The layout is simple and rectangular, following the precepts of the

Catholic Counter-Reformation which demanded an unobstructed layout that enabled the priest to be seen and heard. Nothing about the rest of the church is simple though. The Church favored a highly ornate style to impress congregations with the power and majesty of the Church. Angels and cherubs are everywhere, about 160 on the frieze alone, plus dozens more on the arches and around the windows. The idea was to fuse heaven and earth in one glorious profusion of color and movement. Notice that there's a slight elevation from the front door to the choir. The visitor should feel as though they are "climbing" towards God.

After their expulsion the Jesuits never returned to "their" church but there are a few reminders of their faith inside. On the walls of the sacristy are portraits of various Jesuit saints. In the Holy Mother of the Rosary Chapel the painting of The Adoration depicts the Jesuit Saint Ignatius of Loyola and Saint Francis Xavier.

A handy paper is available inside with detailed descriptions of the chapels and artwork. *(open daily for visits except Sunday)*

Retrace your steps on rue Droite, heading south and in a few meters turn left onto rue du Chateau. Climb up the stairs, noticing the **Galléan coat-of-arms** at 1 rue du Chateau over the entrance to the Acchiardo restaurant. Near the top on the left is an entrance to La Semeuse, a cultural and recreational center within the walls of the former

(33) Jesuit College. It's a mammoth building that runs almost to the Jesuit church, Eglise du Gesù. The Jesuits received permission to establish a college here in 1607. Local religious authorities were opposed to the project but civic leaders liked the idea that local students could be educated in town. To give an idea of the level of educational ability: in 1626 the teaching of Logic was suspended for a year because the pupils couldn't keep up.

By 1665 there were 300 students but the Jesuit right to teach was abruptly revoked in 1729. The building lodged troops during the Revolution and then became a seminary until 1825. It was an art school until La Semeuse took over the premises in 1904. Although the interior has been overhauled, the vaulted halls remain and are easily visible from the entrance on rue du Chateau or around the corner on rue de la Condamine.

Make a left on rue de la Condamine. The name refers to the fact that the street was part of a tax-free zone (condamine) that was under the jurisdiction of the Saint Pons Abbey. Its religious origins are evident at **No 14** which displays medallions of Saints Peter, Paul and John. At No 13 you'll see the

(34) Medieval lintel, which dates from 1485, making it the oldest lintel in Nice. The monogram "IHS" refers to the Latin phrase *Iesus Hominum Salvator* (Jesus, Savior of Man). To the left of the acronym is a floral motif with a fleur-de-lys and on the right is a rosette. The Savoy cross on the far left was probably engraved later. The inscription underneath gives the date of the carving (*1482 die 12 februarii*) and the artist (*barthus ben Pinnxit*) which is interpreted to mean "Barthélémy Bensa painter". It may have once been on a painted surface.

Continue on rue Condamine to rue Rossetti. Look right and you'll see the **Jules Eynaudi stairs** which lead directly to the Colline du Chateau. For centuries this was the main route that linked the Colline with Vieux Nice.

Make a left onto rue Rossetti which leads down to the Cathedral (discussed below). It was enlarged to allow the dead to be carried from religious services in the Cathedral up to the cemetery on the Colline du Chateau. Continue down to the rue Benoit Bunico which was

Nice's Jewish quarter, once known as the rue de la Juiverie. For a time the street was locked at the corner of rue Rossetti and rue de la Loge to the north.

In 1612 the Duke of Savoy, Charles Emmanuel I, issued edicts encouraging wealthy European Jews to settle in Nice with a view towards bolstering the town's finances. Conditions for Jews were good in the 17th century. They could live in the ghetto or not, as they chose. They could freely exercise their religion without stigma, buy and sell property and enter into commercial arrangements with Christians. The Jewish presence was so profitable for the town that Charles Emmanuel II established the port of Villefranche to welcome Jewish immigrants and facilitate their import-export business.

Alas, the acceptance of a Jewish community depended on the goodwill of the Catholic church which cracked down hard in the 18th century. In 1773 Victor Amédée II made living in the ghetto mandatory and Jews had to return to the ghetto after the evening Ave Maria. They were obligated to wear a special robe and a yellow hat. Conditions in the ghetto were miserable and unsanitary.

To regain their freedom of movement, the Jewish community built a network of tunnels that connected them to the rue Droite, outside the ghetto. The tunnels still exist and may have been used as bomb shelters during WWII. Now they lie under private property and are boarded up.

After much local pressure, King Charles Emmanuel III eased restrictions in 1750, allowing Jews to live where they chose. Many moved to the neighborhood around the Port Lympia.

From 1750 through the French revolution Nice's Jews enjoyed substantial freedom but the restoration of the monarchy in 1814 consigned Jews to the ghetto once again. Some obliged, some didn't, probably waiting for the wheel of fortune to turn again. Finally in 1848 a municipal counselor in Nice, Benoit Bunico, insisted on eliminating laws confining Jews in the ghetto. King Charles-Félix agreed and also granted Jews full political and civil rights.

Turn right on rue Benoit Bunico to see the building that hosted a

(35) Synagogue at No 18. Not much is left of the
original building except a plaque commemorating the date of the synagogue's construction in 1733 on the third floor of a building owned by the Black Penitents. In 1886 the synagogue was moved to rue Deloye.

Retrace your steps a block and turn left onto rue Droite. Continue up rue Droite. Notice the **lintel** at No 21. One of many lintels in Old Nice manifesting a belief in divine protection, this one reads "Spes Mea Devs" or "My Hope is in God". Continue to No 15 and the spectacular

(36) Palais Lascaris, an outstanding example of a
Genoese baroque palace. Built as a residence for Jean-Paul Lascaris in the middle of the 17th century, it remained the

property of the powerful Lascaris-Vintimille family until 1792 when they fled to escape Revolutionary forces. Much of the lavish interior decor dates from a restoration in the 1960s. The City of Nice purchased the property in 1942, restored it and turned the palace into a museum. In addition to the frescoes, stuccoes, paintings and sculpture, the Lascaris Palace also displays an important collection of ancient musical instruments.

Just a (free) glimpse of the entrance hall with its colorful ceiling frescoes, arches and sculpture whets the appetite to see more. Climb the wide, balustraded staircase and prepare to travel back to the 18th century. In this world the music is plucked out on beautifully carved wooden instruments. Local notables stare from elaborately framed paintings. Scenes from the Bible or Greek mythology adorn walls and ceilings trimmed with gilt.

On the first floor, one room is devoted to musical instruments such as a serinette, a spinet, violins, harps, mandolins and a lyre. The opposite room displays portraits of the family and local royalty.

Consistent with Genoese style, the second floor is the *piano nobile,* which contains the opulent residential and reception rooms. Despite the Flemish tapestries, delicate instruments and classical art, the compact rooms with soft lighting and high ceilings create a warm, intimate atmosphere. It's as though the architect was balancing the need for a soft, relaxing space with the desire to show off the family's wealth.

It takes about an hour maximum to visit the palace and there are detailed explanations in English of each room. *(open 10am-6pm Wednesday to Monday)*

Across the street from the Palais, notice the unusual building at

(37) No 14 which combines three facades. The lintel over the entrance says *Justice Judex* or "God is my Judge". This 18th-century building is a historic monument.

Continue up the street a few steps to the rue de la Loge. On the left is a

(38) Turkish Cannonball fired during the siege of 1543.

Make a right on rue de la Loge to the

(39) Chapelle de la Sainte-Croix, on rue Saint Joseph, a White Penitents chapel. The Brotherhood moved here in 1761 and the chapel was renovated between 1765 and 1767 by the noted Nice architect Antoine Spinelli (1726-1819) who also designed Place Garibaldi. The elegant facade manages a harmonious combination of Neo-classic and baroque style. Notice the sculpted pelican over the door which symbolizes charity.

The simple floor plan of juxtaposing rectangles is lavishly embellished with floral motifs. The artistic highlight is the cycle of 17th-century paintings devoted to episodes from the life of Jesus. One curious feature is the fresco of the Eternal Father with a globe in his left hand.
(open Tuesday afternoon)

Turn the corner at the rue de la Croix, left of the church, for a beautiful

(40) Frieze of two Penitent brothers on either side of a cross at No 4. Notice that the penitents are wearing conical

53

hoods with eye slits in a jarring reminder of the Ku Klux Klan. It's a *capirote* and it evolved during the Spanish Inquisition. For centuries the *capirote* gave the Penitents anonymity but it is no longer worn. The old facade, which was part of the Chapelle de la Sainte-Croix, has been aggressively renovated but fortunately the frieze remains.

Return to the church. Turn right, retracing your steps along rue de la Loge to the rue Centrale. Turn left and it becomes rue Mascoinat (which means "bad cuisine" in Nice's local dialect). At No 7 note the

(41) Plaque

commemorating the arrival in Nice of the Knights Hospitallers better known as the Knights of Malta. Expelled from the island of Rhodes in Greece in 1522, the Knights wandered Europe for eight years before finally settling in Malta in 1530. During their homeless years, the Knights made this neighborhood their headquarters from 1527 to 1529.

Continue on to the

(42) Place Rossetti,

Nice's liveliest square and the heart of Vieux Nice. In 1825 Rossetti of Chateauneuf donated a plot of land to the city. The city tore down the houses and created this square intended to be large enough for religious processions to gather. Between the Cathedral, the graceful **bell tower** (1731-1757), a central fountain (1980s) and soft ocher facades, it's a particularly pretty place to hang out. Locals and visitors love to spend hours over drinks in one of the cafes just people-watching. Why not pick up some ice cream at famous **Fenocchio**? It's known for its hand-crafted ice cream in unusual flavors such as rose, lavender, tomato and beer.

On the north side of the square is the pharmacy at 15 rue de Pont Vieux which dates from the 18th century and is the oldest **pharmacy** in Nice. On the southern end of the square at 3 rue Sainte Réparate is the marble entrance to the 18th century **episcopal palace** with a "broken pediment" over the door. Inside is a remarkable baroque stairwell.

The highlight of Place Rossetti is the

(43) Cathédrale Sainte Réparate, the largest

sacral building in Nice and the center of the city's religious life. If it's an important wedding or funeral, a major religious holiday or commemorative event, it's bound to happen here. After the 2016 terrorist attack in Nice, the remembrance service was held here.

The story of the church begins with Reparata, a 15-year-old Palestinian virgin martyred in 250AD. First they tried to burn her alive but a miraculous rain doused the flames. Then they made her drink boiling pitch but she still refused to renounce her faith. At that point she was decapitated. A dove appeared to accompany her soul to the afterlife.

According to legend, Nice fishermen soon noticed a wooden ship in the bay piloted by a dove and accompanied by angels. Inside was a young girl wrapped in a white shroud and lying on a bed of flowers. The fishermen hauled the boat to shore and placed the body under a tree. Some say the event gave the bay its name, Baie des Anges (Angel Bay).

In the 11th century a chapel was built for the saint. It became a church in 1455 as the cult of Saint Reparata was growing throughout Europe. In the late 16th century it became a cathedral and eventually Saint Reparata became the patron saint of Nice.

When the population moved down to the *ville basse* in the 16th century it was apparent that a new cathedral would be necessary to accommodate a growing population. Plans for a larger cathedral were entrusted in 1649 to architect, Jean Andre Guibert. He designed it in the shape of a Latin cross with a **cupola** topping the transept. Work proceeded sporadically from 1650. The ominous collapse of a vault in 1658 killed Nice's bishop but the workers pressed on.

The church was finally consecrated in 1699. The bell-tower arose in 1757, a new facade was built in 1830 and lateral aisles were extended in 1899. On the facade is a statue of Saint Reparata, surrounded by the other venerated saints in Nice: Syagre, Bassus, Pontius and Valérien. The same saints adorn the choir. Within the altar are relics of the five saints.

Why five saints? Since the Middle Ages local people were beset by serial catastrophes: plague, cholera, typhus, floods, famine, war, even a strange butterfly infestation (1623). It was more efficient to pray to a bunch of saints at once! It didn't help protect the population against the plague of 1467 which provoked 7800 deaths or the plague of 1631 which resulted in 10,000 deaths.

The interior is a smorgasbord of religious, spiritual, political and local imagery. The saint's initials "SR" is an often-repeated motif. Throughout the nave and the choir, look for the initials of the Savoy princes.

The **high altar** built in 1685, features a central painting representing the Glory of Saint Reparata. Under her left arm is a view of the Colline du Chateau. On the right, is an anonymous painting of Saint Pontius dating from around 1655 which displays (next to his left hand) a view of the

Paillon valley, the Cimiez monastery and the Saint Pons abbey.

The lateral chapels are sumptuously decorated, largely paid for by rich *Niçois* families and businesses. Each chapel has a small explanatory sign in multiple languages.

Left of the entrance is the **Chapel of Four Crowned Martyrs**, which was financed by the masons. The four martyrs were Claude, Nicocastre, Symphorien and Castor, martyred under Diocletian because they refused to sculpt a statue of Aesculapius. The martyrs were venerated by masons and Freemasons. The painting contains masons' tools such as a level, sledgehammer and trowel and Freemason symbols such as a compass and triangle.

Next up on the left aisle is the **Chapel of Saint Reparata** with graphic depictions of her martyrdom. The chapel dates from 1670 and was financed by the Torrini de Fougassières family whose palace stands on the Place du Palais. Their coat-of-arms (a tower with a star over it) is on the bottom right of the central painting and at the top of each of its columns. A glass repository contains the saint's relics.

Don't miss the ornate **Chapel of Saint Rosalie and the Virgin** also on the left aisle. It was built in 1699 to venerate Saint Rosalie of Palermo who protects against the plague.

Each year on October 8 Saint Reparata's feast day is celebrated with processions and a special mass.*(open 9am-noon and 2-6pm Tuesday to Sunday; 2-6pm Monday)*

Take rue Francis Gallo to the right (facing the church). Look up to the left for a view of the **cupola** and its varnished Genoese-style tiles. Continue to rue Colonna d'Istria to look at some interesting

(44) Lintels. Turn left and at No 7 is a Cross of Jerusalem probably linked to the presence in Nice of the Knights of Saint John of Jerusalem. Retrace your steps and on the right is No 8, a lintel from 1649 with the monogram "CHS" (Christus Hominum Salvator).

Return to rue Francis Gallo, turn right and you'll come to the

(45) Porte Fausse. The "False Door" is on the site of what was a private house in the 19th century whose owner allowed the townspeople to use his hallway as a shortcut to the Paillon river (now the Promenade du Paillon). When he died in 1946, he left the house to the city with instructions that it be transformed into a proper gate.

The fountain dates from 1830 just after the city opened a new pipeline to bring water to central Nice from its source in the Pasteur neighborhood. Before then, the Paillon river was the only water source. And who needed it more than the butchers on rue de la Boucherie? Just a few meters away was the city slaughterhouse. Butchers washed the innards of cows and sheep (*tripes*) in this fountain which is why it became known as the *Fountaine aux Tripiers*. When Old Nice entered a period of decline at the turn of the 20th century, people intending to leave for a better neighborhood said they would "*passer la Porte Fausse*". Over the fountain is a sculpted eagle, the symbol of Nice.

More recently, it was artist **Sarkis** who designed this flashy new entrance in 2006.Titled *Les postes restantes de la Porte Fausse*, the multi-colored marble and gold pattern is meant to evoke postcards and letters from around the world. The inscription "Poste Restante" over the fountain alludes to a local tradition that persisted well into the 20th century.

People would write down wishes and prayers and deposit the slips of papers into a slot in the old gate whimsically named Poste Restante. It had to stop because tourists mistook the slot for an actual mailbox.

From Porte Fausse turn right (facing the fountain) and continue east on **rue de la Boucherie.** Clothing shops have now replaced most of the slaughterhouses and butcher shops that once lined the street but a few highly popular shops remain. Up until the 18th century, it was the only place the state authorized to sell meat. In the 19th century the street was devoted to locksmiths and iron workers. Notice the medieval doors at **No 8**.

Rue de la Boucherie becomes rue Collet which was once where tanners worked hides into leather, no doubt dumping the refuse into the Paillon river. Continue on rue Collet which becomes rue Saint-François.

Take a right on rue Sainte-Claire. Near the corner of rue Saint Croix notice the

(46) Palais Caissotti de Roubion, with its striking marble entrance-way. This 18th century palace had belonged to a rich and influential Nice family. Their coat-of-arms, once over the door, was destroyed, probably during the Revolution.

(47) Couvent de la Visitation on Place Sainte Claire. This extensive convent is the oldest in the region, dating to the late 17th century. The order of Clarisses once inhabited the space which included a chapel, cloister and vast garden. Currently the convent is being remodeled into a five-

star hotel over the vigorous objections of the local community.

Make a left onto rue Jouan Nicola and continue to the

(48) Chapelle de la Visitation Sainte-Claire,

a beautiful church built by the Clarisses sisters at the beginning of the 17th century. Notice the scrupulously detailed trompe l'oeil facade. Nice artists Patrice Giuge and Marc Lavalle came up with the remarkable neoclassical design, modeling it on the 19th century frescoes inside. Notice the portraits of Saint Claire and Saint Joseph on either side of the entrance. The insignia on the left is of Monseigneur Lefebvre and on the right the coat-of-arms of Nice.

Retrace your steps to take rue Guigonis downhill, on the right. You'll notice that the street is relatively wide for Vieux Nice. This part of town was overhauled as part of the restoration projects of the 1960s. Go downhill to the rue Saint-François and turn right to the

(49) Place Saint-François, one of Nice's most

historic squares. In 1251 the Franciscans settled here, building a convent and a church. A community developed around the Franciscan settlement as people descended from the Colline du Chateau (Castle Hill) after the siege of 1543.

In 1574 the Palais Communal was constructed to house the Hôtel de Ville (town hall). It lasted until 1792 when the French revolutionaries swept through and pillaged it. The stately building later served various municipal purposes including as a barracks, cinema and ice house before it became the headquarters of the CGT, a powerful labor union. In 1938 fish mongers set up their stalls and the square became known for its fish market.

The buildings were left to crumble until a massive renovation started around 2009. In rehabilitating and excavating the buildings archaeologists discovered arches, caves and even the remains of an early 20th-century cinema. The labor union was evicted and parking was prohibited but the fish market remains. When the renovations are finished the old buildings will house exhibition spaces and a museum of Old Nice. The fountain at the center is *Aux Dauphins,* created in 1938 by Nice sculptor Francois Aragon.

At the northern end of the square is an archway marking the entrance to a vast renovation project that took place in the 1960s. Architect Michel Dikansky supervised the project ensuring that the new structures were built in traditional Nice style but with a pleasing variety of facades.

From the Place Saint-François take rue Pairolière at the eastern end to rue Saint Augustin and make a right, following the sign "La Treille". At No 9 notice the

(50) Maison de La Treille with a luxuriant vine cascading down the building. Treille means "vine" and this one has been here at least since the turn of the 20th century. At one time it was a tavern and then it became a center for Nice's language and traditions. Around 1930 artist Raoul Dufy depicted the house in a painting, *Le Mai à Nice* which now hangs in the Musée des Beaux Arts.

Across the street at No 5 rue Francois Zanin a **lintel** dating from 1636, marks the former Sainte Croix hospital, founded by the White Penitents.

Follow the street to the right of La Treille and you'll come to Place Saint Augustin and

(51) L'Eglise Saint Martin-Saint Augustin,

one of Nice's most original churches. The interior is in an ellipsoid shape rather than the standard rectangular shape.

Its turbulent history began in 1424 when it was built by the hermits of Saint Augustine on the site of an older church. The church was rebuilt between 1683 and 1689 and then rebuilt in the fashionable baroque style between 1716 and 1719. It passed to state control after the French Revolution only to become a barracks in 1821. The church is still owned by the Ministry of Defense.

The earthquake of 1887 destroyed one of the bell towers and another renovation in 1895 gave the church its current look. Martin Luther celebrated a mass here in 1510 and legendary general Giuseppe Garibaldi who created the Kingdom of Italy was baptized here in the *Chapelle Saint Jean-Baptiste* in 1807.

There's plenty to admire in the baroque interior-- polychrome marble, gilt, statues and stucco-- but the highlight is the frescoed vault created in 1828 by Joseph Toselli, a Piedmontese painter. *(open Tuesday afternoons)*

Don't forget to pay homage to Nice's very own heroine at the

(52) Catherine Segurane Monument just

across from the church. It was during the siege of 1543 that the legend of Catherine Segurane was born. The story was that on 15 August 1543 brave Catherine, a washerwoman, mounted the fortress with her laundry stick and beat down a Turkish standard carrier, capturing the Turkish flag. She then lifted her skirts and wiped her bottom with the flag. The prim Turks were so repulsed, they turned tail (so to speak) and fled. A legend was born.

Whatever the truth of the matter, Catherine Segurane became a folk hero for capturing the spirit of Nice. Her monument is placed just where she committed her defiant deed, on the remnants of the old Sincaire bastion. Each year on 15 August there's a procession here and a ceremony in the Saint Martin-Saint Augustin church.

In case your dream was to join the French Foreign Legion go a few steps down the street to No 2 rue Sincaire which is their recruiting center. Otherwise, go down the steps of ruelle Saint Augustin to the left of the church. At the bottom you'll come to rue Pairolière. Just ahead is the

(53) Tour Saint-François, looming 50m high. It

was built along with the Franciscan church and convent but rebuilt many times over the centuries. The current structure dates from the beginning of the 18th century and reflects the baroque influences of the era. The tower has recently been restored and can be visited. The old staircase is visible but too dangerous to climb so it was replaced with a modern staircase. Climb to the top for the city's best view. What a great way to end a tour of Vieux Nice!

(open Wed-Sun 10am-1pm, 2-5.30pm)

Porte Pairolière: the fortified entrance

OLD TOWN MAP

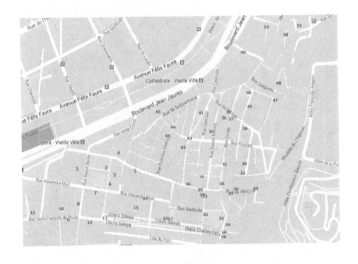

Map Key

1. Palais Corvésy
2. Palais Rusca
3. Place du Palais de Justice
4. Palais des Spitalieri de Cessole
5. Spaggiari Window
6. Cafe du Palais
7. Palais Héraud
8. Cave Bianchi
9. Opéra de Nice
10. Eglise Saint-François de Paule
11. Hôtel de Ville de Nice
12. Palais Hongran
13. Cours Saleya
14. Palais de la Préfecture
15. Musée de la Photographie
16. Chapelle de la Miséricorde
17. Palais Grimaldi
18. Palais Caïs de Pierlas (Matisse House)
19. Chapelle du Saint Suaire
20. Nice Sénat (Centre du Patrimoine)
21. Lintel
22. "Adam & Eve Fresco"
23. Palais de Pons Ceva
24. Eglise Sainte Rita
25. Loggia
26. Stone House
27. Lavoir
28. Governor's House
29. Notre Dame du Malonat
30. Palais des Gallean du Chateauneuf
31. Lintel
32. Eglise du Gesù
33. Jesuit College
34. Medieval lintel
35. Old Synagogue
36. Palais Lascaris
37. No 14
38. Cannonball
39. Chapelle Sainte Croix
40. Frieze
41. Plaque
42. Place Rossetti
43. Cathédrale Sainte Réparate
44. Lintels
45. Porte Fausse
46. Palais Caissotti de Roubion
47. Couvent de la Visitation
48. Chapelle de la Visitation
49. Place Saint-François
50. Maison de la Treille
51. Eglise-Saint-Martin-Saint-Augustine
52. Monument Catherine Segurane
53. Tour Saint-François

Colline du Chateau to Port Lympia

Start Foot of Colline du Chateau (Castle Hill)

Finish Port Lympia

Time 3 hours

Good for History, scenic views, parkland, architecture, kids

Points of Interest ruins of 5th-century Cathedral, Cascade, Cemeteries, Monument aux Morts

Points to Note Start the tour in the morning when the steps up Castle Hill are in shade.

Nice's Port Lympia is a port but there's no chateau or castle on the Colline du Chateau or "Castle Hill". It's a park with unforgettable views over Nice. It's a historical site that tells the story of Nice from its founding to the present day. It's an archaeological treasure trove that is still being excavated. And, with an extensive playground in the center, it's a great place for kids.

The hill that towers over Nice's eastern end defines the city's landscape and is an essential stop to understand and appreciate the city's eventful history. Finishing the walk at Nice's colorful port takes Nice's story up to 2019 when Port Lympia was refurbished to welcome a new cross-city tramway.

HISTORY

The story of the hill begins at least as far back as the Bronze Age around 2100BC, maybe further. Around the third century BC the hill became a Greek colony trading with the Greek settlement of Massalia (now Marseilles). The hilltop settlement became known as Nikaïa.

From the time that Julius Caesar conquered the region in 49BC to the fall of the Roman empire in 476, the hill was continuously occupied although power gravitated its rival, Cemenelum on Cimiez hill. Only nominally under Roman control, the settlement retained strong cultural and commercial links to Greek Massalia. As the ruins of the Cathedral date back to the 5th century, it's clear that the inhabitants were early converts to Christianity.

By the 11th century the settlement expanded to include churches, convents, a market and towers. A second Cathedral was built as well as the first walls to protect the new town.

Documents refer to the hill as a "castrum" or "fortified place" in Latin.

As the town grew and prospered the population spilled down the western slopes of the hill. A new and larger wall that encompassed the eastern part of Vieux Nice was built to protect them. The seat of power was the Chateau at the highest point of the hill. As the administrative center, the Chateau included the town hall and the residence of the governor.

In 1388 Nice became part of the House of Savoy. By that time the town was an important trading post, especially for salt, which prompted the Dukes of Savoy to protect their possession with more walls. In 1436 they increased security by building towers. There were four towers including Saint Elmo tower, rebuilt as the Tour Bellanda.

In the early 16th century new defensive structures arose which included north walls, gates, semi-circular bastions and a well to bring water from below. After a Franco-Turk naval force besieged Nice in 1543, Savoy Duke Emmanuel Philibert decided to turn the whole upper section into a citadel. All civilians moved down to the Old Town and Savoy engineers got to work building more and better fortifications.

Throughout the entire 16th and 17th centuries additional bastions and defensive structures were built. Nevertheless, the French army laid siege in 1691 and once again in 1705. The city capitulated in 1705 and in 1706, the fortress crumbled under relentless artillery fire. Soon after, King Louis XIV razed the entire fortified structure.

During the rest of the 18th century the Princes of Savoy used the hill for military drills and storage. There was a little grazing and a little farming but not enough to stop the occasional landslide that buried the houses below. Barracks and military buildings dotted the landscape until 1934.

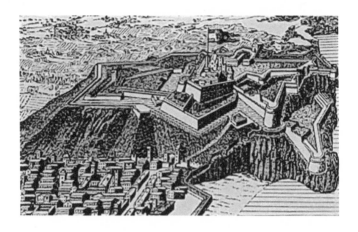

In 1822 the King of Sardinia transformed the hill into a public garden. Botanists replanted the terrain with Aleppo pines, cypresses, oaks and various hardwood trees. As Nice was beginning to flourish as a winter holiday spot for the European aristocracy, the timing was good. Visitors came to stroll the shady paths and enjoy the spectacular views over the Baie des Anges. Installation of the waterfall in 1885 encouraged the growth of more vegetation and more visitors.

With the outbreak of WWII, the Chateau once again regained its military purpose. During the Italian occupation (1940-1943) the top of the hill was bristling with artillery. The Italians also worked on expanding the bomb shelter at the entrance which had been started by locals a year earlier.

When the Germans arrived, they vastly expanded the military installations. They reopened the 16th-century well (now the elevator) and used it to transport munitions and equipment to the top of the hill. They cut down trees and installed mortars, flamethrowers, machine guns and artillery pieces at the top. They tore up the stone steps to make blockhouses. In the final days of the occupation as the Allies advanced, the Germans opened fire, raining bombs and mortar on the buildings below. Twelve people were killed.

Based in the Hotel Suisse next door, the German occupiers also constructed a tunnel system that began across from the elevator where Italians were working on a bomb shelter. One tunnel led to the port and another led to the beach. The door to the port tunnel is visible next to the Monument aux Morts and remains of the beach exit are visible at the Bains de la Police beach across from the steps. Both exits were equipped with antitank weapons and ammunition storage depots. The entrance next to the elevator was fortified with a blockhouse.

Much remains unclear about the Germans' intended use for the tunnels. Some say they intended to use the beach outlets to launch U-boats but documentation for that assertion is sparse. One non-military use for the tunnels was to store an elaborate metal staircase from the celebrated Casino de la Jetée that the Germans destroyed to melt down the iron. (see the Promenade des Anglais walk). After the war the tunnels were sealed although the entrance is visible next to the elevator.

Archaeological explorations of the Chateau began in the 1950s and revealed the ruins of the ancient cathedral. Much of the top of the hill was transformed into a vast playground and sports center. It seems that each new administration in Nice brings new ideas for embellishing castle hill. Who knows what the future will hold?

Start your exploration at the

(1) Foot of Castle Hill (1 rue des Ponchettes) where

an **elevator** (if it's in service) can whisk you to the top of the hill in a minute. At the end of a short tunnel built by the

German occupiers, the elevator occupies the exact spot of a 72-meter well that once brought water from a subterranean stream to the hilltop. As there's no natural water source at the top of the hill, inhabitants were forced to build cisterns to gather rain water. Finally in 1517 a Sardinian engineer, Andre Bergante, figured out how to pump water up to the Chateau from a water source at the foot of the hill. It was considered a magnificent feat of engineering and was named the "eighth wonder of the world". People even whispered that Mr. Bergante must have had help from Satan to construct such a thing and began calling it the *puits du diable* or "devil's well".

The well was used until the destruction of the Chateau in 1706 but reopened during the French Revolution before being definitively closed in 1830. The elevator was installed in 1952.

Stroll across the street to the Promenade. Look west across Castel beach to the

(2) Bains de la Police. The concrete platform is all that remains of the Nazi-built blockhouse that forms the entrance to the tunnels underneath the hill.

Return and next to the elevator entrance are the

(3) Lesage steps, built in 1888 to allow easier access to the gardens being planted on top. There are 426 steps but it's a pleasant climb with a number of platforms to rest and enjoy the view. The west-facing steps are cool and shady in the morning and the overhanging trees and shrubs provide some protection against the afternoon sun.

At the first landing is the best view of the

(4) Bellanda Tower, the circular tower that punctuates the end of the Promenade des Anglais. It occupies the site of the former Saint Elmo tower which formed part of the lower defensive walls of the citadel. Saint Elmo was the patron saint of sailors.

Built in 1436 to protect the Chateau's western flank, the Saint Elmo tower was destroyed by Louis XIV in 1706 and lay in ruins for over a century. Around the middle of the 19th century Honoré Clérissi bought the site and built the current tower as part of his hotel below. He suspected that the panoramic view of the Baie des Anges would attract the celebrated foreigners flocking to Nice for their health. He was right.

Among the most famous residents of the "Clérissi Tower" was the composer Hector Berlioz. In 1831 Berlioz stopped in Nice en route to Paris where he planned to murder his fiancée who broke off the engagement to marry another man. Equipped with two pistols, a maid's costume as a disguise and some poison as a backup in case the pistols misfired, the distraught composer changed his mind under Nice's glorious sunshine. Instead, he stayed in Clérissi's hotel in a room with a sea view. Entranced with the view and the sound of the waves he regained his mental health. The Paris murder trip? Canceled!

While there, he composed the overture, *Roi Lear* based on Shakespeare's play. Thirteen years later Berlioz found himself ill with stress and exhaustion and again found the cure in Nice. He returned to Bellanda and started work on the overture, *Le Corsaire,* which he originally named *La Tour de Nice.* A plaque commemorating his stay is on the second landing.

The Bellanda tower became part of the Hotel Suisse in the early 20th century. The Germans used it as a gym during their occupation of Nice which left it in pitiful condition. The City of Nice repaired it in the 1950s and turned it into a naval museum. Now it houses the **Bellandarium,** a small, free museum with dioramas and explanations of Castle Hill's history. *(open Saturday 10am-1pm and 2-6pm).*

Continue up to the third landing for a

(5) Panoramic view from the top of the tower that takes in all of Nice and the mountains beyond. An orientation table identifies the topographical features and a tower viewer allows you to take a closer look.

Continue up the stairs. At the fork, turn right following the "Panorama" sign and a few steps further is the

(6) Tour de la Place d'Armes which was built around 1640, destroyed in 1706 and rebuilt in the 19th-century. The base of the tower is original and a few stones are from the ramparts that once linked it to the Bellanda Tower.

You're almost there! Another flight of stairs takes you to the top. Turn right and there's **La Citadelle** snack stand, tables and chairs. A sign reminds you that this was the

(7) Upper Platform, the earliest known settlement probably dating back at least to the 11th century. It was converted to public gardens in 1828.

(If you've opted for the elevator, take the stairs on the left after the exit, then go left on the road to the top. To your left is a sign "Tour Bellanda" and stairs leading down to the Tour de la Place d'Armes and Bellanda Tower.)

Take the road straight uphill from the sign "Upper Plateau" with the pond on your left. On the right is a grassy field and just beyond is the

(8) Cathédrale Sainte Marie, the hill's most

significant archaeological site. The first sacred structure here dates back to the 5th century. Little is known about it except that it was a 22m by 10m rectangle. During the 8th and 9th century an apse was constructed but it was not until the 11th century that a recognizable church emerged with two apses and columns arranged in the style of a typical medieval church. In the beginning of the 12th century, the clergy arrived along with a nave and choir. In the 15th century the church was enlarged on the eastern side and became Cathédrale Sainte Marie (Saint Mary's Cathedral). The church lasted until its destruction in 1706.

Around a large holm oak tree are remains of the side chapels. Go up to the platform where signs on the right offer a visual reconstitution of the church as it originally appeared. Notice the remains of two large pillars in the church nave. Two column bases delineate the choir. They belong either to the 11th-century church or to the second medieval cathedral. Two semi-circular apses and a chancel screen are still visible. Low walls around the pillars are vestiges of the 5th century church. Archaeologists are still excavating the ruins of another old church dedicated to Saint John the Baptist and a clerical cemetery nearby.

Go up the stairs at the end of the platform and you'll be in the evocative

(9) Arcades, erected in the postwar period as part of an overall refurbishment of the park. Admire the **mosaics** mounted in 1970.

Facing the mosaics, head right and then down the paved road. About 25 meters further on the left are ruins of the

(10) Military Warehouses, indicated by a sign. These 16th-century structures were positioned between the cathedral and the north wall.

Continue down the route and notice the **cathedral choir** on the right.

Continue down the same road to a circular ground mosaic dedicated to Ulysses with the reminder: "Happy are those who, like Ulysses, had a beautiful voyage". Turn left to a

(11) Lookout point with a sweeping view over the port to the neighborhood of Mont Boron and Fort Alban which was also part of Nice's defense system.

Go back up the same road with the cathedral ruins now on your left. Across from the mosaics is a sign marking the semi-circular platform that corresponds to the former

(12) Saint Charles Tower. Built in 1517, this 12-meter-high tower was a key part of the Chateau's defensive system that included the Saint Paul tower to the east and the Saint Victor tower to the west. Originally known as the *Tour de Malebouche*, there was an access ramp that led to the tower's gate, *La Porte Ducale.* Saint Charles Tower is in the center of the illustration below.

Continue a short distance to the asphalt esplanade at the foot of the old

(13) Chateau, built sometime between the 13th and 14th century. You are looking at the walls of the old palace, known as a "castrum". which was both an administrative and residential center for the ruling class. At one time it was protected by a double wall and a tower that has since disappeared. A sign indicates the spot where a **cannon ball** left its mark.

At the top of the walls is **Le Point de Vue** a casual restaurant for light refreshments (cash only).

Go up the stairs on the left of the restaurant to the **Heart of the Chateau.** Notice that this is the highest point and offers a panoramic view. Whoever was governing at the time had this view from his apartments. Centuries later, in 1860, Napoleon III came to visit and exclaimed 'It's the most beautiful landscape in the world!"

It was from this spot that Nice's **midday cannon** was once fired. Have you noticed a loud boom at noon? Now, a firecracker does the trick but at one time an actual cannon fired to mark midday. The tradition began in 1863 with

Thomas Coventry a wealthy English lawyer accustomed to wintering in Nice. Although legend has it that he had the cannon fired to remind his chatty wife to return from her morning walk and make lunch, the real story is more complicated.

At the time, every gentleman needed a hobby and for Mr Coventry that hobby was measuring time. And, as a civic-minded person, he decided that Nice residents needed better timekeeping. First he funded a sundial on the southern facade of the Nice Opera House and then he built a clock in the arcades of the Place Masséna. To set the clock he installed a red time ball on the roof of his hotel nearby, modeled on the one in Greenwich. At 11.55am each day (except Sunday) he hoisted the ball to the top of the pole which signaled his artillery man to fire the cannon at noon.

After his death, the tradition lapsed for a few years but popular demand insisted upon its return and the cannon began booming again in 1875. The boom at noon continues to this day. But watch out on April Fools Day. The firecracker intentionally goes off at the wrong time!

Go back down the stairs and take a sharp right on the road downhill. Take the first right to the

(14) Gate and Underpass which are the only remains of the old Chateau and served as a point of access to the heart of the medieval palace above. Go down a little bit to pass under a **Gothic arch** rebuilt in 1876 with stones from the medieval gate.

Return to the path and go left a few steps to the

(15) Cascade, a lush and refreshing oasis built under the shadow of an old fortified tower. In the late 19th-century the Chateau was undergoing a transformation into a recreational area. What better place to commemorate the new water system that brought water from the Vesubie valley, about 50km north of Nice, to the Cascade and the city of Nice? The Cascade was inaugurated 27 June 1885.

Take the stairs at the far end of the Cascade and go straight ahead to the platform which is the top of the

(16) Saint Victor tower. The tower is a 19th century reconstruction of the original tower built in 1517. The center of this platform corresponds to the central axis of the original tower which had a diameter of 24m.

Go down the stairs to see the vestiges of the original tower and a

(17) Plaque of Eugene Emanuel (1817-1880), a lawyer who devoted his retirement to writing songs and poems in *Nissart*, Nice's local dialect. The plaque is on the **Ramparts** that once linked the Saint Victor tower to the Saint Charles tower.

Follow the route to the cemetery. After the turn, take the stairway to the left indicated by a

(18) Sign (*direction cemetières/Vieille Ville*) and stop at the grassy patch of land containing vestiges of the

(19) Citadelle to the right. This unimpressive wall fragment is in fact one of the rare vestiges of the citadel's western wall constructed between 1577 and 1579. It was then surrounded by the bastions constructed a little before the siege of 1705.

Take the stairs down from the platform and turn right. About 50m on is the

(20) Justes parmi les Nations a slab of granite, marble and concrete erected in 2014 to memorialize the 125 Righteous men, women and children of the Alpes-Maritimes who acted to save Jews from the Holocaust. The honorific "Righteous among the Nations" was created by the Holocaust remembrance society Yad Vashem based in Israel to honor non-Jews who risked their lives to save Jews during the Holocaust. The monument is bordered by two panels, "lieu de mémoire" displaying texts from philosopher Simone Veil.

A few meters further a sign reminds you that this road was once the

(21) Moat. It was bordered to the south (on the right) by the two bastions which protected the northern front in the 16th century.

Return in the opposite direction and go down to the crossroads.

Bear right to the

Cemeteries, undoubtedly the most beautiful burial grounds in Nice. Up until the late 18th century Nice's dead were buried either in Vieux Nice or, if they had the money, in one of Nice's churches. In 1783 King Victor Amadée III decreed that, for hygienic reasons, church burials were forbidden; henceforth all burials were to be outside the city center. As the Colline du Chateau was little more than a vast, empty area it seemed the natural place for a cemetery. Plus, there were a lot of stones lying around from the 16th-century citadel which were used to create the cemetery walls. The Christian cemetery opened in 1783 and the Jewish cemetery, which had been on rue Sincaire in the Old Town, was moved just south of the Christian cemetery shortly thereafter.

You'll first come to the

(22) Jewish Cemetery. To the left of the entrance is a wall inscribed with the names of 3602 men, women and children deported from Nice to the Nazi death camps. Jews from the entire region and Monaco were rounded up and held in Nice. The deportations began slowly in 1942, paused between November 1942 and September 1943 under the Italian occupation and recommenced with vigor under the German occupation. Between September 1943 and August 1944 over 3000 Jews were either deported or shot on the spot.

Enter the cemetery and on your right is a **commemorative wall** erected by the Jewish community in Nice. The left side commemorates the heroes of the resistance with an urn containing ashes of those who perished in the Auschwitz death camp. On the right a panel commemorates the martyrs of persecutions with an urn containing human grease that the Nazis fabricated from the dead.

Notice the unusual **tombstone** directly opposite adorned with a train, plane, car and pine tree sculptures. It is a tomb of a seven-year-old boy who asked his parents for his favorite items. Unable to comply with his dying request at the time, they honored his wishes in death with this moving testament to parental love.

The oldest tomb in the cemetery dates from 1540. Most of the oldest stones are near the entrance. The most notable tomb is that of famed jeweler **Alfred Van Cleef** to the left in the first row.

Go down further to the **Chapel of the Holy Trinity,** built by architect Francois Aragon in 1935 near the entrance to the

(23) Christian Cemetery, a testament to the
remarkable cultural, historical and artistic diversity of Nice and one of Europe's great monumental cemeteries. There are 2250 Catholic, Protestant and Orthodox tombs in an exuberant mixture of artistic styles. The oldest tombs date from the first half of the 19th century and exhibit a neoclassical style. Most of the tomb art goes farther afield displaying busts, medallions and statues of the deceased, symbolic motifs such as crosses, angels, anchors and flowers, lots of crying maidens and the occasional horror movie tableau.

Don't miss the **Gastaud family tomb** where the angel of death hovers over a tomb half-opened by stone hands. The Gastaud family once owned most of west Nice as a result of Andre Gastaud's shady machinations after the Revolution (see the West Nice walk).

There are tombs of all social groups from the unknowns of Vieux Nice to political and artistic notables to the Russians, Poles, Germans, English and Americans who flocked to Nice at the turn of the 20th century.

There's a map at the entrance as well as QR code activated explanations (in French). The caretaker's office across from the entrance is another helpful source of information. Here are some notable tombs:

Pyramid, erected to the victims of the Opera fire of 1881

Emmanuel Danelle family, topped by a nude that scandalized society

Rosa Garibaldi, mother of Garibaldi, the Italian general

Alexander Herzen, a statue of the "father of Russian socialism" tops the tomb

Marguerite Matisse, daughter of the famous painter (buried in Cimiez cemetery)

Leon Gambetta, the French statesman

Gaston Leroux, author of "The Phantom of the Opera" and other works.

François Grosso, a civic-minded business-man and philanthropist whose extraordinary 12-meter high tomb displays his wife and two children topped by a benevolent angel.

Emil Jellinek, the automobile entrepreneur who founded the Mercedes brand which he named after his daughter.

Ilhami Hussein Pasha, a former Prime Minister of Egypt whose tomb is a masterpiece of Islamic art.

Upon leaving the cemetery go right and head downhill. The walls to the right were constructed with remnants of the 16th-century citadel walls. Continue down to the

(24) Moat covering which may have been the northern limit of the citadel.

Take the long walk downhill to the exit and bear right to the

(25) Monument aux Morts inaugurated in 1928 as a monument to the 3665 Nice citizens who perished in WWI. Planning for the project began at the end of 1918 almost immediately after the armistice. Tucked into an old quarry whose stones furnished the walls of Nice port, the monument is austere and modern. The architect was the Nice-born Roger Seassal (1885-1967) who won the Grand Prix of Rome and Alfred Janniot (1889-1969) took charge of the sculptures. It's considered a masterpiece of Art Deco design.

The central urn, dignified and majestic, is inscribed with the names of WWI military campaigns and below are the names of the Nice soldiers who died in combat. Within are the identification tags of the fallen *Niçois*. The five steps leading up to the urn symbolize the years from 1914 to 1918. Slabs bordering the forecourt are ornamented with bas-reliefs representing the different army branches.

Each year on November 11, Armistice Day, a remembrance ceremony takes place here.

Before moving on, don't forget to notice **green door** to the right of the Monument next to the restaurant. The green door is an entrance to the tunnel system crafted by the Germans in WWII.

Across the road is the intriguing **Croix de Mission**. The wrought iron cross tops a marble pedestal with the Latin engraving "In Memoriam Jubilaei 1829 et Pacis 1871". Erected in 1829 to commemorate the jubilee of an unidentified religious event, the reference to 1871 was added later to commemorate the peace following the Franco-Prussian war of 1870. Notice that the surrounding structure is designed as an altar facing the sea. It was to this spot that the annual Procession of Rogations headed each spring to pray for divine protection of the countryside.

Retrace your steps heading east and begin your exploration of the

Port Lympia, one of Nice's most enticing and photogenic spots. The sun's slanting afternoon rays perfectly illuminate the multicolored buildings on the eastern side.

Until the mid-18th century the whole port was little more than a swamp fed by a water source named Lympia. All marine traffic used the small and inadequate beach-port, Ponchettes, that lay just outside the old town. The lack of a proper port was hampering the economic development of a rapidly expanding town.

Casting around for a solution, King Charles Emmanuel III had the ambitious idea to turn the Lympia marshland into a port and began working on the project in 1748. For building materials he used some of the rubble left by Louis XIV destruction of the Chateau and for workers he used the galley slaves that were lodged in the nearby penal colony (*bagne*), now the Caserne Lympia.

Creating an artificial port proved to be more complicated and costly than expected and work proceeded slowly. Also, the kingdom was chronically indebted due to its incessant wars. Meanwhile, a new neighborhood was constructed with roads that would link the port with the road to Turin that ran along the Paillon river. Place Garibaldi to the north and Place Ile-de-Beauté became the centerpieces of a lively new commercial and residential neighborhood. The Jewish community that was no longer confined to the old town ghetto settled the neighborhood and opened businesses. Construction of the actual port languished and halted entirely when French Revolutionary forces invaded in 1792.

It wasn't until 1831 that work began in earnest and lasted for the rest of the century. The port was enlarged and modernized which led to the destruction of many buildings from the previous century. Most of the buildings around the port were completed in the late 19th-century and display a pleasantly harmonious style. Warehouses, mills and factories set up shop ready to handle Nice's bustling import-export trade.

Still, much to the disappointment of city planners, Nice's port was and is outclassed by the much larger commercial ports of Marseilles and Genoa. The port remains too small for giant cruise ships which head to Villefranche-sur-Mer instead. Every so often a mayor advances the idea of expanding the port to attract cruise traffic but the old port seems just too pretty to tear down.

Right at the entrance to the port on quai Lunel is a

(26) Statue of Charles-Félix, the Sardinian king

who was determined to complete the port project. Local merchants commissioned the statue in 1826, grateful that the king had promised to preserve the port's status as a *port franc* (duty-free zone). Notice that the king is pointing toward the port. His popularity was short-lived however. The port lost its status as a duty-free zone in 1853 which was a serious economic blow. Furious *Niçois* rioted and broke the index finger of the statue. Small wonder that in 1860 Nice voted to leave the House of Savoy and become part of France.

Look way across the port to see

(27) The Applevage Crane. So what, you say? It's just an old crane, you say? This crane is a historic monument. This crane dates from 1938. It was one of two cranes commissioned to handle the unloading of coal at the port. The other crane was destroyed in 1952 but this crane stands as the port's last remaining machinery. The name of the company that built it was Applevage.

Stroll up the quai Lunel and look for the

(28) Lou Passagin sign on the quai. The beloved Lou Passagin service is a free shuttle that runs between the eastern and western quays. It initially began as a way for retired fishermen to supplement their income by transporting passengers in their traditional fishing boats, the *pointus*. The service still uses *pointus* but brought up to date with the installation of solar-powered electric motors that can be recharged at the dock. It's a quiet, ecologically efficient and altogether delightful way to traverse the port. The service runs continuously from 10am to 7pm during the tourist season.

Hop aboard the boat for the five-minute trip to the eastern quay. At the dock, note the fleet of ***pointus*** to your left. Although no longer used for fishing, their owners carefully maintain their boats. Ahead and to the right is the

(29) Caserne Lympia at 2 Quai Entrecasteaux with its striking clock tower. Now a museum and cultural center, the Caserne Lympia dates back to the earliest days of the port construction. In 1750 it was a prison that housed the galley slaves who worked on the port. It also contained warehouses for the construction equipment.

In 1826, King Charles-Félix decided to improve the living conditions of the prisoners and guards by enlarging the grounds. He built two pavilions at each end of the building including the clock tower in the north. It served as a prison until 1887 and was then used as an army barracks (*caserne*) before being renovated and transformed into a museum and cultural center in 2017.

Visits to the small museum must be booked in advance but a quick tour of the renovated facade makes its previous incarnation as a prison vividly clear.

Hop the boat back to quai Lunel where you'll see a number of places to grab a drink or a bite to eat. Most are open for lunch and dinner service only but **Le Lunel** is open all day.

Proceeding up quai Lunel notice the

(30) Palais de la Marine at number 22. Built

between 1781 and 1784 this elegant porticoed building was originally intended to house the captain and the port services. Notice the anchor motif worked into the wrought iron balcony. Today it is the Directorate of Maritime Affairs.

And then the

(31) Maison Liprandi at No 20. Dating from 1751,

this building is one of the oldest on the port and beautifully displays the prevailing Turinese style.

And then note the

(32) Douane (Customs Building) at 4 quai de la Douane (yes, same street different name) which was built in 1950. The neoclassical Turin-style facade is inspired by the buildings on Place Garibaldi.

Keep going to browse the

(33) Marché aux Puces flea market on Place Robilante. Paintings, vintage furniture, lamps, bric-a-brac; you never know what you'll find.

The flea market has only been here since 1995. It began shortly after WWI as a series of stalls along the banks of the Paillon river (now boulevard Risso) and was meant to help war widows, orphans and veterans earn money. It was strictly regulated. To get a place a seller had to be native *Niçois*, listed on the voter rolls and provide proof of financial difficulty. In those days everyone from countesses to *clochards* to actresses looking for unusual get-ups came to shop there.

As a series of projects beginning in 1931 covered over the river, the sellers moved further downstream along the boulevard. By the 1960s the question of where to relocate the stalls became pressing. The antique dealers along nearby rue Segurane wanted their rivals as far away as possible. For a while they had a space in front of the Monument aux Morts but they complained that it was too hot and sunny.

Finally this attractive little flea market village was constructed especially for them in 1995 and they've been here ever since.

(closed Sunday, Monday)

At the northeast corner of the port, notice the

(34) Birthplace of Garibaldi at 2 quai Papacino, memorialized on a plaque. The original building was destroyed in 1880, during the expansion of the port.

Turn right and you're at the **Place Ile-de-Beauté** marked by the

(35) Eglise Notre-Dame-du-Port. The first stone was laid in 1840 for a new church but the structure collapsed before it could be completed. A new church opened in 1853, destined to serve the maritime community. It wasn't until 1896 that the neoclassical facade with columns was completed. The church is also known as *l'Eglise de l'Immaculée Conception*.

On either side of the church are the

(36) Palais Astraudo and Malbéqui which continue the neoclassical look. To the west of the church is the palace of the rich oil merchant, Pie Astraudo which dates from 1844; the Malbéqui Palace to the east wasn't completed until 1890. Local lore has it that the Malbéqui Palace brings bad luck probably because of the name (*mal*=bad, *bec*=mouth). It's said that no business thrives there. Each building is a superb example of the Turinese penchant for symmetry though. The ocher facades are adorned with bas-reliefs, colonnaded arcades and balconies. What appear to be ceiling medallions are entirely trompe l'oeil.

Cross the street and in the middle of the two roads is a

(37) Dog bar. This green cast-iron fountain was a gift from New York's Society for the Protection of Animals in 1901 to the immense relief of Nice's thirsty canine population.

Cross over to the

(38) Monumental staircase built under French rule in 1889. Intended to allow fishermen and maritime workers to easily access the city, it now serves as a stairway to tram line 2 which opened in 2019.

Before hopping on the tramway, take a look at the

(39) Sculpture "Lou Che". This 14-meter high steel sculpture by Noël Dolla is intended to represent "three boats which sail on the Mediterranean". It was installed with the opening of the tramway line 2 in December 2019. Locals were not pleased and quickly gathered 700 signatures on a petition to tear it down. For whatever reason, their complaints were ignored. Lou Che is still standing.

19th-century prisoners laboring to build the port

CASTLE HILL - PORT MAP

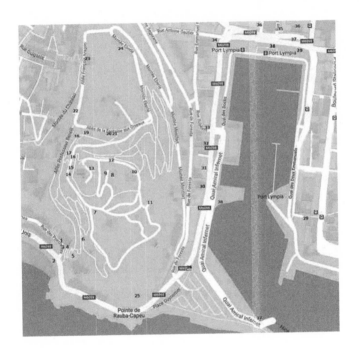

Map Key

CIMIEZ:
FROM ROMANS TO ROYALS

Start Cimiez/Hôpital Nice

Finish Bibliothèque Romain Gary

Time 3 hours

Good for History, art, archaeology, Belle Epoque architecture

Points of Interest Roman baths & Amphitheater, Franciscan Monastery, Matisse Museum, Chagall Museum, Archaeological Museum

Points to Note Museums are closed Tuesday

Y̶ou could say that Nice's early history was a tale of two hills: Nikaïa (Colline du Chateau) to the south and Cemenelum (Cimiez) to the north. They were both settled at about the same time but evolved differently. The Colline du Chateau reached its apogee as a military fortress in the 16th century while the glory days of Cimiez occurred during its tenure as a Roman city and again during its rebirth into a royal holiday spot in the 19th century.

Unlike the Colline du Chateau, Cimiez is densely inhabited. With its wide boulevards, vast park and spectacular Belle Epoque apartment buildings, it's long been the chicest and most prestigious neighborhood in Nice.

HISTORY

Cimiez's story begins with the ancient Ligurians who occupied the hill for centuries before the Romans arrived in the 1st century BC. It was a good spot for a military outpost as it was far from the sea and close to the route linking France and Italy. It may have been the Ligurians who first referred to their settlement as Cemenelum which the Romans adopted as the name of their military outpost here.

After they subdued local resistance, the Romans made Cimiez the provincial capital of *Alpes maritimæ* in the 1st century AD. In addition to building aqueducts to supply their city of about 10,000 with water, the Romans built an amphitheater (now the Arenas) and public baths.

In the 4th century the Romans extended their reach to other regions and Cemenelum's importance declined relative to its ancient rival, Nikaïa. People drifted away, leaving only a few farms. The ancient Roman city fell into ruin, its stones used for building materials or covered in weeds.

In the 9th century the Benedictine order that had established a renowned monastery, Saint Pontius, on the eastern side of the Cimiez hill built a small church on top of the hill. In the 16th century the Franciscans took over that church and built a monastery.

The Franciscan Monastery was surrounded by farmland and gradually Nice's affluent families began building holiday homes on the hill. The 17th century Palais Gubernatis that now houses the Matisse Museum is an example.

Cimiez's fortunes changed dramatically in the 19th century. First, the dry hill was connected to a water system which made it more livable and easier to cultivate the land.

Real estate developers were quick to see the potential for cashing in on Nice's growing reputation among European aristocrats for clean air and a healthy lifestyle. A consortium led by star architect Sébastien Marcel Biasini (1841-1913) laid out the grand boulevard de Cimiez, developed the land and sold off plots to be developed into luxury hotels, villas and apartment buildings.

Then, when Queen Victoria chose Cimiez as her favorite holiday spot in 1895, the neighborhood rocketed to the top of everyone's "must visit" list and never looked back. Architects outdid themselves in creating splendid buildings that offered the most modern amenities to attract the cream of European nobility. The winter season was a round of balls and dinner parties, concerts and exhibits.

The outbreak of WWI put an end to the fun. Some of the grand buildings were turned into military hospitals and most had to be renovated after the war. Guests returned but not in the same numbers. Many found themselves in straightened circumstances, particularly Russians after the Russian revolution. The decline continued during the crash of 1929 and WWII.

Cimiez's grand hotels were also confronted with changing tastes. Seaside holidays became increasingly popular and Nice developed a summer season. The hotels were turned into luxury apartments and many of the old mansions were torn down and replaced with apartment buildings. As you stroll the streets you'll notice that the prewar buildings have tiny balconies (if any) while the postwar buildings have large balconies to accommodate the new taste for taking in the sun. Fortunately enough older buildings remain to conjure up the days when Cimiez was the European epicenter of grace and elegance.

Start your walk at

(1) Cimiez Hospital which was once the **Grand Hotel de Cimiez** 4 ave Reine Victoria. Notice the name of the street? Here is where Her Majesty Queen Victoria stayed for six weeks in 1895. She had already visited several other destinations on the Riviera but Nice was the only spot she visited more than once. Built in 1880, the Grand Hotel was a massive five-story Belle Epoque hotel with a 28,000 sq meter park that was considered the height of luxury at the time. The Queen and an entourage of 50 stayed in an annex, the Hotel Vitali, which she rented for 40,000 francs. She liked it so much that she returned in 1896 for another six-week stay before shifting her loyalties to the Excelsior Regina Hotel.

It's easy to enter the grounds for a close-up look at the handsome architecture by Aaron Messiah (1858-1940). Just inside the main entrance is an impressive marble and wrought iron staircase.

Continue down ave Reine Victoria 100m or so and turn left on ave Regina which is entirely devoted to the

(2) Excelsior Regina Hotel 71-73 boulevard

Cimiez. When Queen Victoria returned for a second visit to the Grand Hotel of Cimiez, developers spied an opportunity to accommodate queenly tastes while boosting the image of Nice. But she was already 75 which meant work had to begin immediately.

The architect was Sébastien Marcel Biasini who began construction in June 1895. Within a year the Queen could contemplate the splendid Renaissance style facade that stretched to 195m. In less than two years the building was finished, divided between a public hotel and a western wing just for Her Majesty.

The Queen had a private entrance under the western tower topped with a queenly dome. By the time she crossed the threshold in 1897 the ultra-modern hotel boasted 400 rooms, 233 bathrooms and three elevators. There was electric lighting, central heating and a modern sewage disposal system. Using the name "Lady Balmoral" as a pseudonym, she paid 80,000 francs for a two week stay in a suite of 70 rooms. Her entourage of 40 included a number of Indians whose outfits provoked immense curiosity among the locals.

During her stays Queen Victoria entertained aristocrats from all Europe. Emperor Franz Joseph of Austria, Queen Wilhelmina of the Netherlands, French President Félix Faure were frequent visitors along with her son, the future Edward VII. The flurry of international journalists that covered the royal presence brought massive and priceless publicity to Nice. Sadly, the Queen's health deteriorated after 1899 and she could no longer make the journey. Shortly before her death in 1901 she reportedly said "Oh, if only I were in Nice I would have healed".

The death of the Queen dealt a severe blow to the hotel and, in fact, to the entire neighborhood. Worse, with the outbreak of WWI the hotel was transformed into a military hospital. A restoration process spruced up the hotel after the war but rich aristocrats were in shorter supply. Nevertheless Winston Churchill, Aga Kahn III and a few other notables came down for short stays. The crash of 1929 dealt a final blow to the illustrious establishment and in 1934 the hotel was transformed into apartments.

The next famous guest was the artist **Henri Matisse** who bought two apartments on the third floor of the Regina in 1938. His space was large enough to include a 300-bird aviary tended by a keeper. With his sweeping views of the Baie des Anges he was inspired to create *La nature morte au magnolia*, *La rose violette* and *La Nymphe dans la forêt* among other works. Matisse stayed in the Regina throughout the Italian occupation, only leaving in 1943 to wait out the war in Vence. Upon his return in 1949, he busied himself with encouraging young artists and setting up a gallery along the Promenade des Anglais. He worked right up until his last days, turning out masterpieces such as the series of Blue Nudes. Matisse passed away in the Regina in 1954.

The Excelsior Regina is a private apartment complex now and cannot be visited but the exterior is a wonder to contemplate. The architect created a Belle Epoque masterpiece ornamented with stucco reliefs, oriel windows and glass canopies. The wrought iron dome over the Queen's apartments was designed by François-Félix Gordolon (1852-1901). Notice the glass, wrought iron and gold-plated ornamentation at the entrance. An ornate marble and metal walkway links the hotel with the 8250 sq meter garden. A marble statue of the Queen receiving flowers from children stands in front of the southern entrance to the garden (more below).

For those determined to glimpse the inside, the 2020 Netflix film *Rebecca* filmed scenes in the Excelsior Regina lobby.

Bear left after the Hotel Regina and across the street next to the bus stop is the entrance to the **Le Jardin des Arènes de Cimiez,** a vast park and garden that includes the Roman amphitheater, Roman baths, Archaeological Museum and Matisse Museum. It was the site of the Nice Jazz Festival until 2014. You'll notice that the paths are marked with the names of famous jazz musicians that played there over its 55-year history.

Another popular festival held here is the *Fête des Courgourdons* which takes place annually in the spring. The festival celebrates the non-edible gourds that have traditionally been cultivated in the region and carved into toys, musical instruments and utensils. There's singing, folk dancing, bands and food stalls.

Right at the entrance to the gardens is the

(3) Arènes, an amphitheater built between 70 and 85AD and then modified a few times until the 3rd century. Its elliptical form could accommodate up to 5000 spectators on its bleachers yet this is considered a relatively small Roman amphitheater. The 7m high structure on the northeast side was used to stretch out an awning to protect the crowds below.

The two monumental entrance ways on the north and south axis were rebuilt in the 1930s. It was through the southern gate, *porta triumphalis,* that the VIPs entered to take their places in the loges to the east and west. The gladiators entered through the northern gate, *porta libitinensis,* which also served to evacuate the wounded and dead.

Contrary to popular belief, the "thumbs up he lives, thumbs down he dies" trope is false. Whatever gestures the public used to determine the fate of a gladiator, these men were expensive to keep and to train and usually were allowed to live and fight another day.

The more likely scenario occurred at the combat between Prothéos and Lantinus under the reign of Emperor Gallien. Empress Salonina was the wife of the Emperor and she came to Cemenelum for her health in 261 AD. She disliked conflict of all kinds and was perturbed by the ongoing rivalry between her Roman city of Cemenelum and the Greek city of Nikaïa on the Colline du Chateau. She decided to organize a gladiator combat in the Arenas to settle the matter once and for all. Nikaïa chose Prothéos, celebrated for his prowess in the ring throughout ancient Liguria. The Romans chose Lantinus, an unknown who arrived completely masked. The two gladiators fought with enthusiasm. At the moment when it appeared that Lantinus was about to fall, the Empress sprang to her feet and shouted "These men shouldn't die. There's no more rivalry between Nikaïa and Cemenelum!". Lantinus took off his mask and the Empress was shocked to discover that it was her own son, Publius Licinius Cornelius Valerianus. The crowd was delighted and everyone poured out of the Arenas to celebrate in the gardens.

Saint Pontius had a sadder fate. This Roman converted to Christianity and began proselytizing in the region. Emperor Valerian sentenced him to be devoured by bears in the Cimiez amphitheater. Legend has it that the bears spared him and Pontius walked away. But destiny had the final word. Three years later he was decapitated by the Paillon river and, they say, his head rolled to the bottom of Cimiez hill. The powerful Saint Pons (Pontius) Basilique on the eastern side of Cimiez hill was erected at that very spot.

Past the amphitheater, signs direct you to the

(4) Musée d'Archéologie de Nice Cimiez

which includes the **Roman baths.** Entrance to the Baths is through the museum, a perfect way to understand the site. Especially evocative are the mock-ups that show the Baths as they once looked. But there's much more. The museum displays objects from ancient Cemenelum as well as the entire region, drawn from archaeological excavations and private collections. Statues, stelae, sarcophagi, vases, dishes, jewelry and more evoke the practical and spiritual life of the ancients. Sculpted hairpins and earrings dropped in the ladies baths are a poignant reminder of beauty rituals throughout the ages. Particularly impressive is the faune dansant, a bronze from the 1st century AD with a remarkably detailed rendition of muscles, hair and beard. The looming statue of Antonia Minor, daughter of Marc Antony and Octavia, is impossible to miss. Multiple panels outline the history of Cemenelum and the Baths (in French).

Pass through the museum to visit the **Roman baths.** For the Romans attendance at a public bath was a social occasion. People discussed the events of the day, flirted, closed business deals and, oh yes, bathed. There were three zones in the thermal baths of Cimiez: North, East and West. The North baths were the first and largest, probably built sometime between the 1st and 3rd centuries AD. All were constructed with brick on the outside and marble walls and floors inside.

Each bath zone contained four spaces: the *frigadarium* (cold bath); *tepidarium* (lukewarm bath); *laconicum* (sauna) in the rear of the *tepidarium, destricatrium* for scraping oil and sweat from the body; *caldarium* (hot bath). Two aqueducts supplied the site with water: Falicon and Mouraille. Drainage pipes emptied into a large basin at the foot of the southern facade of the East baths.

The North baths are the most complete of the thermal complexes. The frigidarium was a 9m by 12m room decorated with polychrome marble walls, marble statues and contained an oval swimming pool. Follow the three heated rooms: the *tepidarium* (which gives access to a *laconicum*, a circular oven), the *destricatrium* and the *caldarium*. The heating system, the *praefurnium,* is located north of the three hot rooms. The North baths was actually occupied by a farm family until the 1950s.

The East baths are smaller but offered the same level of luxury. The heating system to the north of the three hot rooms is well-preserved. To the north of the buildings is a pool.

At the end of the 5th century, Christians settled the West baths and transformed it into a cathedral and baptistery. It was the first settlement of Christians in Nice. Remains of the *frigidarium* and *caldarium* are still visible and were probably used in baptism rituals. The discovery of an earring and hairpins in one of the basins led to the speculation that this zone was for ladies.

(open 10am-6pm Wednesday to Monday)

Right next door to the museum and baths is the

(5) Musée Matisse, housed in a stately 17th century Genoese-style villa. Painted in cheerful red tones and decorated with trompe l'oeil windows, it had belonged to the

105

Gubernatis family before becoming a hotel at the end of the 19th century.

Matisse's first works dating from 1890 to 1905 are displayed on the ground floor of the villa. Noticing his "first" painting, *Nature Morte aux Livres* and various copies he did of works found in the Louvre provides an invaluable starting point for understanding Matisse's progression.

Matisse's stay in Nice is memorialized in his masterpieces *Tempete a Nice* (1919) and *Odalisque au Coffret Rouge* (1926). Also notice his most famous paintings from the 1930s which include *Fenetre a Tahiti* and *Nymphe dans la foret*.

An entire room is dedicated to the cut gouaches the artist created in later years as his physical health declined. Also interesting is the collection of studies Matisse executed in preparation for his magnificent stained glass in the Vence chapel.

Another room is dedicated to the ceramic *La Piscine*, a gift from Claude and Barbara Duthuit in 2013.

Throughout the museum, the life and personality of the artist emerges through displays of the objects he painted as well as family photographs.

In addition to the permanent collection housed in the villa, a series of temporary exhibitions are mounted in the villa's modern wing.

(open 10am-6pm Wednesday to Monday)

Follow signs to the

(6) Monastère Franciscain on the other side of the park. First the Romans erected a temple to the goddess Diana on this spot. The four steps to enter the church come from the remains of the Roman temple. Then the Benedictine order arrived in the 9th century to build a church

and monastery. By the 16th century their church, *Sainte-Marie des Anges*, and monastery had fallen into disuse.

The Benedictines were looking to sell and the Franciscan order was looking to buy following the destruction of their Old Town monastery during the Ottoman attacks of 1543. After taking possession in 1546 the Franciscan monks' first job was to sink a well. Providentially, an old Roman aqueduct, fed by Falicon to the north, happened to pass right their terrain. Lucky break. Word spread that the monks could provide fresh, clean water to visitors. And so visitors came, often bearing gifts.

Next, they erected a small cloister with monk cells next to the dilapidated old church that remained from the Benedictine days. Over the years they repaired the church and about a century later built a larger cloister. The generosity of the local nobility allowed them to expand the church and install their treasures.

Their most prized treasures from their former monastery included three masterpieces from Nice artist Louis Bréa (c1450-1523). Working with his brother, Antoine, Louis Bréa bridged the Middle Ages and the Renaissance with scrupulously detailed religious paintings. The monastery possesses *La Crucifixion*, *La Pietà* and *La Déposition de Croix*. *La Pietà* is to the right of the entrance. Only a copy of *La Crucifixion* is on display; the newly-restored original is currently in the Masséna Museum. *La Déposition de Croix* is also on display but could use a restoration.

Consecrated in 1667. Sainte-Marie des Anges was adorned with a massive carved **wooden altarpiece**. Rooms, corridors and staircases were ornamented for the monks and the monks began acquiring paintings. In the 18th century the large outer cloister was built as well as an entrance gate.

In 1697 the brothers acquired the skeletal remains of Saint Victoria which added to the church's prestige. Victoria was the daughter of a rich third-century Roman and sister to Saint Anatolia. Both young women refused to marry their chosen fiancés because they were pagan. Drama ensued and a burst of legends. Supposedly the two sisters were imprisoned and tortured before being executed. Victoria's remains were extracted from a cemetery in Rome and given to Count Gubernatis who donated them to the monastery. **Saint Victoria's skeleton** is displayed on the church's left aisle.

Revolutionaries seized the monastery in 1793, turning it into a barracks and then a military hospital. In 1816 King Victor Emmanuel, the Duke of Savoy, returned the property to the Franciscans.

After regaining possession of their monastery the monks set about restoring, improving and redesigning their property. The astonishing **western facade** was rebuilt in 1845 in troubadour style with slender steeples. On each side of the door are inscriptions relating the history of Cimiez. Inside, the painter Hercule Trachel decorated a vault with frescoes illustrating the Assumption while the Florentine painter Giacomelli decorated the choir and the nave with paintings celebrating Franciscan saints.

One of the most precious treasures is the *Croix Séraphique* sculpted in 1477 that depicts Christ with wings. The Seraphic Christ of the sculpture refers to Saint Francis' vision of Christ while he prayed on a Tuscan mountain. Depictions of Christ with wings are exceedingly rare. Next to the right hand is a representation of Saint Francis of Assisi. Next to the left is Saint Louis of Toulouse, a Franciscan saint. On top a pelican nourishes three babies, a symbol of charity. At the foot is the coat of arms of the Sardina family that helped finance the refurbishment of the statue after the Revolution. A copy stands outside the entrance to the Cemetery.

There is also a small **museum** on the 2nd floor that depicts the daily life of a Franciscan monk but it is currently closed.

(open 9am-6pm Thurs-Tues)

Outside the church and monastery are the splendid

(7) **Monastery Gardens.** Gardens are essential to monastery life not only for cultivating food but also for its symbolic value. For monks, everything that grows in a garden is a gift from God that links the monastery to the Divine. The garden is a reflection of Eden that embodies Divine beauty and perfection. Monastery gardens are organized in checkerboard style with sections devoted to herbs, food plants, flowers and trees.

The monastery gardens of Cimiez are the oldest gardens in Nice and certainly the most scenic with sweeping views over the region. There are orange trees, lemon trees, olive trees, magnificent magnolias, cypresses, oaks, climbing roses and other flowers.

At one time the monks grew a variety of greens that they combined into *mesclun* salad, a Nice specialty. Each morning a monk would assemble a mixture of rocket, dandelion greens, burnet, chervil, chicory and watercress. He would place the salad in two large baskets, descend to town on a mule and distribute it to the townspeople. They were also known for a homemade soybean sprout salad served with mustard seeds.

Turn left immediately after the entrance, pass under the pergola and you'll come to an elaborate **vertical sundial** dating from 1876 outside the entrance to the cloister. The cloister is typically closed but opens on some summer evenings for classical music concerts.

A staircase on the right of the main garden as you proceed to the end leads to the **Ligurian oppidum**, a wall that dates from somewhere between the 4th and 1st century BC when the Ligurians had settled the hill.

Adjacent to the monastery is the

(8) Cemetery, a veritable museum of 19th-century funerary art.

Until 1783 the aristocracy was buried in churches while the common people were relegated to a common ditch. The King of Sardinia, Victor Amédée III changed all that with an edict ending church burials. Signs direct you to the most famous resting residents of the cemetery: Raoul Dufy and Henri Matisse. Although they had become estranged in life, Matisse's wife, Amélie, is buried with him.

Less famous but still noteworthy is the tomb of Samuel L. Goldenberg, an American lace importer who, with his wife, Nella Sondheim, made regular trips to the Riviera for health reasons. On April 10, 1912 the couple boarded the *Titanic* at Cherbourg as first-class passengers back to America. Both were rescued from the sinking ship two days later but the trauma left him temporarily blind. The couple divorced and Mr Goldenberg then married Edwige Garbowska, a Polish countess with property in Nice. They settled in a villa in Cimiez and devoted themselves to an association for the blind, based in Nice's old Sénat building. The countess died in 1935 and Mr Goldenberg died in 1936.

Retrace your steps back through the park and turn left onto **boulevard de Cimiez**. A short way down on the right you'll come to a

(9) Statue of Queen Victoria. Sculptor Louis Maubert (1875-1949) created the statue in 1912 as an homage to the queen. Made out of gleaming white marble, this fine sculpture depicts the kindly queen receiving flowers from four young girls intended to represent the four towns Queen Victoria visited: Nice, Cannes, Grasse and Menton. It was once in the Excelsior Regina's gardens but is now here at the southern end.

Cross to the other side of boulevard de Cimiez and turn left on **boulevard Edouard VII** for a series of gorgeous villas that have remained mostly intact after their construction. The street was named after Edward VII, Queen Victoria's oldest son who made many trips to Nice. The first villa is

(10) Villa Guelma at No 13, built in 1909. Unfortunately the villa is almost entirely obscured by hedges and a gate but here is where the painter Raoul Dufy (1877-1953) lived with his wife Emilienne from 1925 to 1929. Emilienne was a native *Niçois*e and Dufy became enchanted with Nice and the sun-saturated Riviera colors. A number of his paintings of Emilienne, the Villa Guelma and Nice are on display in the Musée des Beaux-Arts.

Next is the

(11) Villa La Perle at No 11 which was built in 1910. Jacques Durand was the architect who designed this stately villa in an Art Nouveau style.

A few doors down is

(12) Manoir Belgrano at No 5. This highly unusual (for Nice) building is a Renaissance mansion designed by Nice architect Charles Dalmas (1863-1938) in 1911. Dalmas was the force behind many of the Riviera's most iconic buildings including the Hotel Carlton in Cannes. The cut stone and brick facade, turrets, gables and twisted columns clearly recall a different age.

The name refers to a neighborhood in Buenos Aires. Perhaps the Argentine owner, Antonio Santa Maria, was homesick? The last owner and resident was the Afghan prince and ambassador to France, Sardar Shah Wali Khan.

The strong wall surrounding the villa made it a secure choice for Captain Geoffrey Jones who helped direct the restoration of civic life in Nice from his headquarters here in August 1944.

Return to boulevard de Cimiez and head downhill. On your right you'll come to the Passage Regina. On the corner is the handsome

(13) Villa Allah Karim at No 59. Built in 1904 for a renowned horticulturist, Michel Falicon, the villa retains its charm even though most of the elaborate exterior decoration has been destroyed.

Keep going on Passage Regina and at the end of the block is the entrance to

(14) Parc Liserb. Although now a gated residential area, the Parc Liserb was once a romantic 85,000 sq meter park dotted with flower beds, ornamental rock gardens, faux ruins, an artificial grotto and the Villa Liserb. A wealthy English businessman, Edward Cazalet, acquired the property

112

in 1870 and passed to his son William in 1883. When Queen Victoria started her annual Nice holidays in 1895, William was ready to welcome her to his villa and park. He even constructed a special wide path for her donkey cart to pass from the Excelsior Regina to his property. Hence, the street name, Passage Regina. To entice her he organized musical evenings with Slavic and Italian musicians.

With the Queen's passing and the agonies of WWI, the villa and park languished until it gained new life as a movie set. *La Sultane de l'amour* (1919)was a 50-minute long black and white silent film (later hand-colored!) that began Nice's reign as a film location (later expanded to the Victorine studios in west Nice). The film is available free and gives a

good look at the Parc Liserb's grounds, past the sliver of splendor you see through the massive iron entrance gates. That same year a much better film also used Parc Liserb in some scenes: *J'accuse,* an anti-war masterpiece by Abel Gance. The Parc Liserb scenes are fleeting however.

Return to boulevard de Cimiez, turn right and at No 57 is the

(15) Palais Tony Pin, a flamboyant Belle Epoque masterpiece. Built in 1906, it was the first of the Belle Epoque palaces built as a residence, not a hotel.

Continue down the boulevard to the

(16) Palais Prince de Galles at No 53 behind gates. Built around 1890 when the English were flocking to Cimiez, this magnificent building was a hotel and named to honor the Prince of Wales, the Queen's first-born son, Edward, who was to become Edward VII.

It's on the corner of the boulevard Prince de Galles, also named after Edward. At the end of the street are the **Neo-Gothic entrance towers** to the

(17) Parc de Valrose. This magnificent 10-hectare estate was built between 1867 and 1870 by Baron Von Derwies. a Russian financier and counselor to Tsar Alexander II. No fewer than four architects were involved in the planning and construction of the Gothic castle and 400-seat concert hall. The vast garden was filled with grottoes and kiosks, exotic plants and statuary. The towers that you see were designed by Sébastien Marcel Biasini.

From 1870 to 1881, Valrose became a hotbed of musical and social life. The finest conductors came to conduct the in-house orchestra and the most celebrated virtuosos of the day came to play for an audience of industrialists and aristocrats.

The castle and park is considered a historic monument and now belongs to the University of Nice. It is not open for public visits.

Next on boulevard de Cimiez is an

(18) Art Deco building at No 51, a little jewel of postwar Art Deco design that makes the other Belle Epoque palaces look overwrought. The building is recognizable by the frieze of carved flowers that runs across the top of the second floor. At the heart of each flower is a seashell. The facade is made up of stones cut in different sizes and shapes and a graceful pediment tops the bow windows.

Across the street is the splendid

(19) Winter Palace at No 82. It was built as a prestigious hotel in 1900 by Nice architect Charles Dalmas (1863-1938) and was the first to have a flat roof. Behind the monumental entrance overlooking a winter garden were palatial rooms outfitted in Louis XVI style and equipped with giant red marble fireplaces. The vast dining room was over what is now a pharmacy. The landscaped park is the size of a small village and once included a tennis court and miniature golf. Like so many hotels, it was transformed into luxury apartments in 1941 but the gorgeous Belle Epoque facade was restored to its former glory in 2010.

Keep going downhill to the

(20) Riviera Palace at No 39 built in 1892 by Nice architect Sébastien Marcel Biasini who also built the Excelsior Regina Hotel. The majestic 110m long hotel opens onto a vast park that has been left largely intact even after

the hotel was converted to apartments in the mid-20th century. It welcomed President Felix Faure on an official visit in 1898 and was the favorite lodging for Prince Nashimoto of Japan. During WWII it served as a convalescent home for American army officers.

Further down is the

(21) Villa Surany at No 35 which was built in 1902. At the time there was a fashion for orientalism which is evident in its horseshoe arches and stunning friezes of earthenware and polychrome mosaics. Architect Adam Dettlopf designed it for Giuseppe Raffaeli but, after court proceedings, it fell into the hands of Herman Back, Count of Surany, Consul of Persia.

During the Italian occupation of Nice (1940-1943), Italian General Lospinoso made the Villa Surany his headquarters. Charged with relocating Jews to the hinterlands, Lospinoso worked with local leaders to transport over 4000 Jews to safety.

Across the street is the

(22) Hotel Alhambra at No 48 behind the Hotel Florida. It's an extraordinary example of Orientalism in the heart of Cimiez with horseshoe arches and minarets rising from a classical facade. Built in 1900, the building is also unusual as the product of a female entrepreneur. Madame Emilie Gabrielle Sabatier, the ex-wife of the Vicompte de Bernis. noticed that hotels catering to foreign tourists were a lucrative investment. She organized a loan, hired Nice architect Jules Sioly to build the structure and engaged a celebrated horticulturalist, Nabbonnand, to design the

gardens. The Neo-Moorish style was a canny way to attract an international clientele enamored with exoticism.

Madame Sabatier went on to develop real estate projects elsewhere and the hotel did a healthy business right up to WWI when it was requisitioned as a military hospital. The few guests that had returned after the end of WWI fled at the outbreak of WWII.

After the liberation of France in August 1944, Major Robert T. Frederick turned the Alhambra into his headquarters overseeing the restoration of order. The following year members of the WAC (Women's Army Corps) were treated to short vacations there.

Like so many Cimiez hotels, the Alhambra failed to recover after WWII. It was transformed into apartments in 1947 and is now classed as a historic monument.

Continue down boulevard de Cimiez to the remarkable

(23) Villa Paradiso at No 24. The first incarnation of the Villa Paradiso was as a residence for a rich businessman, Adolf Sicard in 1881. Towards the end of the century architect Constantin Scala overhauled it into a handsome residence for Baron Etienne Van Zuylen and his wife Helene, the daughter of Baron Salomon and Adele de Rothschild. Helene was a prominent lesbian and author who also was the first woman to compete in an international motor race. The couple were highly invested in animal welfare and created the Nice chapter of the Society for the Protection of Animals. Each year they held a garden party here to benefit animals. Guests enjoyed "best in show" competitions for dogs and cats, dogs doing tricks and raffles. The proceeds went to animal rescue operations.

The Van Zuylens lived on the property until WWII when it was rented to Countess Gurowski-Massé. She welcomed Prix de Rome scholars who were no longer able to stay in Mussolini's Rome.

The city of Nice acquired the building in 1943 and renovated it to house the Conservatory of Music which has since moved. After a misbegotten attempt to sell the property, it will now be refurbished to house various local associations. Currently it's easy to walk onto the property and admire the architecture.

Cross the street and right on the corner of avenue Docteur Menard is the

(24) Chagall Museum, dedicated to the works of

Marc Chagall (1887-1985). It's one of the few museums where the artist himself had a hand in its design. Chagall loved the region and moved to nearby Vence in 1950. It was there that he created the Biblical Message cycle, composed of 17 large paintings on Old Testament themes. His donation of these paintings to France inspired the creation of this museum.

In 1970 architect Andre Hermant began construction of the museum with substantial input from the artist. Chagall wanted the building to be a place of spirituality, not exactly a museum and not exactly a chapel but a serene environment for prayer and meditation. The clean, sober lines of the building and oblique lighting keep the focus on the master's vivid colors and striking forms, just as he wanted.

As the project took shape, Chagall requested the addition of an auditorium and ornamented it with stained-glass windows depicting the creation of the world. The auditorium shows a documentary film that acquaints visitors with Chagall's life and works during the day and serves as a concert hall on occasional evenings. Chagall decided how the paintings were to be exhibited and even created a new wall mosaic, *The Prophet Elijah*, especially for the museum.

Chagall also worked on the design of the garden with Henri Fisch. The trees are Mediterranean: olive, cypress, pine and green oak. White and blue flowers predominate and the African lilies are set to blossom on Chagall's birthday, July 7.

The museum opened in July 1973 on Chagall's birthday in the presence of the artist himself. Chagall participated in the museum's exhibitions and events for the rest of his life. *(open 10am-6pm Wednesday-Monday)*

Continue on avenue Docteur Menard for a block and you'll come to

(25) Pagode Tu Quang at No 32. This tiny pagoda represents the school of Vietnamese Mahayana and has been serving the Vietnamese Buddhist community in Nice since 1976. It's open for visits on Sundays and is known for the home-cooked vegan lunch it offers the first Sunday of the month.

Return to boulevard de Cimiez and continue down the right side of the street. In the far distance you can see the belvedere of the **Villa Rezian,** built in 1911. Continue to the

(26) Palais de Valence at No 15, an example of the Art Deco style in Cimiez, built in 1928. The style is particularly evident in the ironwork on the doors and the stucco over the windows. Also notice the trompe l'oeil on the northern side of the building.

Not too much farther downhill is

(27) Le Majestic at No 4, a building which perfectly
illustrates its name. Built between 1906 and 1909, the
"Majestic Palace Hotel" was the brainchild of architect Jules
Fevre who was an early adopter of Art Deco style. Financed
by Swiss investors, Mr Febvre was able to think big. Behind
the impressive entrance topped by two square towers lie 400
rooms. He also thought luxury. Half of the rooms were built
with private bathrooms (still a rarity in France at the time)
and elevators whisked guests up the six-story building.
France's most famous female writer, Colette, stayed here in
1911. The venerable old hotel is now a luxury apartment
building but many of the Art Deco interior decorations have
been preserved.

The early 20th-century construction frenzy culminated in

(28) Le Grand Palais at No 2. All nine floors of the
building were completed in 1912, which was a record.
Architect Charles Dalmas had the innovative idea to pose the
masonry facade over a steel structure. The **Petit Palais** next
to it is an annex to the main building.

In a further nod to its elite clientele, the hotel had its
own little funicular that ran from 4 avenue Désambrois near
the bus stop. It was only 70m away from the hotel but it
spared the guests the inconvenience of mounting a slight
slope.

Although built as hotels, both the Grand and Petit Palais
are now luxury residences.

Continue down the hill a couple of hundred meters to
the

(29) Greek Orthodox Church of Saint Spyridon, at 2 avenue Désambrois. The Greek community in Nice bought an old villa in 1953, refurbished it and consecrated it in 1957. Behind the iron gate lies a relaxing garden of stone, exotic plants and mosaics. Inside, the vaults and walls are covered with splendid Byzantine frescoes from the Cretan school on a background of 22 carat gold. Painter Lazaros Zikos of Athens contributed the work in 1992. When the sun filters through the stained glass windows illuminating the iconostasis, the effect is startling and deeply spiritual. The church also serves as a cultural center and language school. In addition to Sunday mornings, the church is open on occasional weekdays. Their website, www.st-spyridon-nice.com, has details.

The red building next door, **Mas de Sablonat,** is popularly known as the **Maison des Nains** (house of dwarves) because of its sidewalk-level windows and entrance door. The unusually low first floor appears to be crushing the first floor, giving the impression that only small people can live there. No, it's not a house of hobbits! The ground floor is partially buried because architect Paul Trachel placed the foundation 1.50 meters underground. The building dates from 1926.

Across the street is the

(30) Palais Jacques Cauvin at 1 avenue Désambrois, notable for the sculpted facade by Michel de Tarnowsky (1870-1946).

Continue along avenue Dubouchage to reach Square Durandy and the

(31) Bibliothèque Romain Gary. This public

library is in the **Villa Rambourg,** built by a Parisian industrialist in 1875. The city bought it in 1923 and instructed city architect Nicolas Anselmi to transform it into a library. Anselmi widened the building and added a top floor but many elements of the neoclassical facade remain. Notice the sundial over the entrance with a Latin inscription that translates as "The iron may well be wrong on the clock, but when the sun is shining I'm not wrong". Walk around to the north side of the building to admire the glass and iron Art Deco entrance.

The Art Deco style is most pronounced inside. The grand staircase is from the original building but the reading room upstairs is the product of Anselmi and decorator Clément Goyenèche who created a bright, rectangular space of clean lines and artful lighting. On the western wall is a painting by Edouard Fer (1887-1959) created especially for the library, titled *Nice inspiratrice des arts et des lettres*. Against the background of the Baie des Anges are three figures: a florist symbolizing Nice gardens, a fisherwoman symbolizing the sea and a shepherdess symbolizing the mountains. In the foreground is a still life displaying the flowers, fruits and vegetables of Nice.

The villa's garden, now the Square Durandy, has been reworked many times since the 19th century but remains a pleasant place to relax. It's free to visit the library which specializes in Nice history. Hours vary but weekday afternoons are a good bet.

Ballroom, Excelsior Hotel Régina

CIMIEZ MAP

Map Key

1 Cimiez Hospital

2 Excelsior Regina

3 Arènes

4 Musée d'Archéologie

5 Musée Matisse

6 Monastère Franciscain

7 Monastery Gardens

8 Cemetery

9 Statue of Queen Victoria

10 Villa Guelma

11 Villa La Perle

12 Manoir Belgrano

13 Villa Allah Karim

14 Parc Liserb

15 Palais Tony Pin

16 Palais Prince de Galles

17 Parc de Valrose

18 Art Deco Building

19 Winter Palace

20 Riviera Palace

21 Villa Surany

22 Hotel Alhambra

23 Villa Paradiso

24 Marc Chagall National Museum

25 Pagoda

26 Palais de Valence

27 The Majestic

28 Grand and Petit Palais

29 Greek Orthodox Church

30 Palais Jacques Cauvin

31 Bibliothèque Romain Gary

PROMENADE DES ANGLAIS: THE BRITISH INFLUENCE

Start Neuf Lignes Obliques

Finish CUM

Time 2 1/2 hours

Good for Belle Epoque and Art Deco villas and hotels, public art and sculpture

Points of Interest Masséna Museum, Marble Cross

Points to Note The Masséna Museum is closed Tuesday

To Nice residents the Promenade des Anglais is La Prom and it's the center of Nice life. It's a gym, running track, seaside stroll, pickup strip, kiddie playground, roller derby, cycling route and fashion parade. It's the place to go for a marital discussion, family outing or a contemplative session of sea-staring. On one side, there's the rippling and blue Baie des Anges and on the other side, well, there's a rippling and busy five-lane road. It's relaxation, urban-style.

HISTORY

The Promenade des Anglais was financed and built by the British who began holidaying in Nice around the end of the 18th century. The splendors of Nice were becoming widely known at the time thanks to Scottish writer and poet Tobias Smollett. He arrived in Nice in 1763, stayed two years and published his pungent observations in *Travels through France and Italy* in 1766.

At first there were only about 80 to 100 families making the journey from London each year and, for the most part, they avoided the malodorous and unsanitary streets of Vieux Nice. After all, they came for their health! Instead they rented houses on the west bank of the Paillon river along the rue de France. A community developed around the marble cross on the rue de France in the neighborhood, *Faubourg de la Croix de Marbre*. Stores selling products from home sprung up and their signs were in English. The English called it "Newborough".

The visitors had a problem however. The only place to take a healthy stroll by the sea was *Les Terrasses,* the elevated promenade in Vieux Nice. Getting there involved trekking to the only bridge over the Paillon river near the Lycée Masséna and then winding their way through the narrow streets of Vieux Nice where beggars pestered them at every turn. Unacceptable.

In 1822 Reverend Lewis Way of the nearby Anglican church launched a charitable drive among his congregants to construct a path along the sea, easily accessible from their neighborhood. The plan not only solved their promenade problem but it gave work to the local population whose poverty they found distressing. Completed in 1824, this dusty 2- meter wide path became the *Chemin des Anglais* and ran only from the Paillon river to rue Meyerbeer.

Meanwhile the Sardinian King Charles Albert decided to modernize his Savoy cities. In 1832 he created an urban planning commission, the, Consiglio d'Ornato, to supervise the construction of roads, squares and parks in the "new borough". With a nod to the "distinguished foreigners" living in the *Faubourg de la Croix de Marbre*, the commission authorized the extension of the *Chemin des Anglais* to the Les Baumettes neighborhood in west Nice. By 1844 the new street was complete. Since the "distinguished foreigners" loved a touch of exoticism, the promenade was adorned with its iconic palm trees. In 1856 the Promenade was extended to the Magnan river.

The opening of the railroad in 1864, made Nice easily accessible to northern European aristocrats. Some built mansions in the Quartier des Musiciens while others stayed in one of the luxurious new hotels along the Promenade. Gas lights were installed along the Promenade for pleasant evening strolls and a bridge over the Paillon extended the Promenade east. The Promenade became the whirring center of the winter season as carriages came and went, the mansions buzzed with balls and aristocrats showed off their finery on seaside walks.

WWI caused visitors to drift away from Nice and some of the grand hotels were requisitioned as military hospitals. With the end of the war visitors returned but this time

it was the summer season that brought them and many were American industrialists. The Promenade was expanded to include a road and extended to Nice Airport. Prominent local architects designed apartment buildings to replace the old villas.

The latest project has been to greatly expand the space given to bike paths which now run the entire length of the Promenade from the port to the airport. The opening of tramway line 2 in 2019 has greatly diminished cross town car traffic and has gone a long way to returning the Promenade to the tranquility that early visitors must have experienced.

Start at the

(1) Neuf Lignes Obliques, or l'Obélisque the monumental steel sculpture by Nice artist Bernar Venet. You can't miss it. The nine 30-meter high steel beams that meet at the top symbolize the nine valleys that converge on Nice.

At least that's what Mayor Christian Estrosi said when the statue was inaugurated in 2010 to commemorate the 150th anniversary of Nice's attachment to France. The artist himself remains mum. It has yet to become beloved among the locals. Some say it disfigures the Promenade. Others reply "And the Hotel Meridien?"

The sculpture is on the **Quai des Etats-Unis** so named in 1917 just after the United States declared war on Germany for which the French were mightily grateful. After the war Nice welcomed droves of American servicemen on leave including the future President Harry Truman in 1918. He found the city "magnificent" and returned in 1958 for a vacation.

The ties between Nice and the United States were memorialized by the **Statue of Liberty**, placed about 150m east in front of the Opera House. Although only a meter high, it's an original statue made by Bartholdi, the sculptor who made the iconic statue welcoming people to New York. As the sculptor typically started with small sculptures that he enlarged, this statue was probably made before her larger sister in 1875. Nice bought the statue in 2011 and installed it in 2014 on the anniversary of WWI.

Cross the street to the Parking Sulzer and admire the

(2) Défly building with an incredible trompe l'oeil facade

on the eastern side of the square. The only real element on the otherwise flat surface is the overhanging gutter on the top. It was built in 1843 for the Défly family whose initials are part of the railing on the first floor balcony.

Behind the building is another trompe l'oeil facade that's also excellent. The railing, chimney stacks and the small window on the top floor are the only real features.

Continue heading west and in a few meters note the handsome

(3) Hotel Beau Rivage.

Built shortly after Nice's attachment to France in 1860, Matisse stayed here on his first visit to Nice in 1917. It was where he first fell in love with Nice and where he painted *Autoportrait*, *Intérieur au violon* and a number of interiors from his room. Although his room was small and dark, the window opened onto a sea view. "What made me stay was the great colored reflection of January, the luminosity of the days," he wrote. Matisse stayed until April 1918 when the hotel was requisitioned by the American army. Chekhov also stayed here in 1891 and 1894. The part of the building facing the sea was transformed into apartments in 1984.

Next to it at

(4) 109 quai des Etats-Unis

is where philosopher Friedrich Nietzsche stayed in 1885 to work on his tome "Beyond Good and Evil". It was one of six sojourns in Nice he made between 1883 and 1888. In addition to working on his books and refining his theory of the will to power, Nietzsche took long walks to the nearby towns of Eze and Saint-Jean-Cap-Ferrat. He probably would have returned in 1889 but he lost his mind to dementia and died shortly thereafter.

On the promenade itself notice the

(5) Chaise Bleue

sculpture by contemporary artist Sabine Géraudi, known as SAB. Nice's blue chairs are an icon of the city. Locals like nothing better than to grab a chair and contemplate the sea. Chairs on the Promenade first appeared after WWII and were painted white. Those white wooden chairs eventually became blue metal chairs and now are joined together to prevent theft.

Across the street is the wide avenue des Phocéens which was once the left bank of the **Paillon river**. As you walk past the **Jardin Albert 1er** on the right (more on the Jardin in the Promenade du Paillon walk) you're walking on what was once the *Pont Napoléon III* and then the *Pont des Anges*. This bridge spanned the Paillon river from 1863 until 1895 when the Paillon was covered from Place Masséna to the sea. Look down to see the Paillon river empty (or trickle) into the Baie des Anges. Storms occasionally turn this deceptively peaceful little stream into a raging torrent crashing down from its mountain source 30km north of Nice.

There's some local controversy about where the **Baie des Anges** got its name. Some say it was when the martyred Saint Reparata drifted into the bay on a boat accompanied by angels. Others insist that it was the fishermen who named the bay after the *ange de mer* or angelfish (Squatina oculata) whose wing-like appendages got tangled in their nets. It's an ugly fish with a toad-like face and skin rough enough to polish wood. Although too bony to eat, the angelfish has become quite rare locally.

Continue west to the

(6) Hotel Meridien which is on the site of the lavish

Hotel Ruhl, built in 1913 and destroyed in 1970, much to the distress of locals. Before the Hotel Ruhl there was the Hotel des Anglais, a splendid Belle Epoque hotel. Although the architecture is unlikely to set hearts aflame the rooftop bar is a great place for a cocktail.

Hotel Ruhl with pavilion leading to the Casino de la Jetée

When locals of a certain age gaze at the sea from the Hotel
Meridien they see a ghostly structure. They see a soaring
pleasure palace that was known as the **Casino de la Jetée
Promenade**. Built in 1891 this splendid steel and glass
structure with a 25-meter high dome, turrets and minarets
quickly became the unofficial emblem of Nice. It was
reproduced on countless postcards, artists such as Dufy were
compelled to paint it, everyone had to see it. Inside was a
casino, concert hall, restaurant, lounges, reading and gaming
rooms. The vogue for "exotic" style was evident in Indian,
Japanese, Turkish and Moorish decorative features. Alas, all
that steel and iron proved too tempting for the Germans
who occupied the city during WWII. In 1944 they
dismantled the structure and used the metal for armaments.
Its disappearance was a blow to the seaside landscape and a
psychic wound that has never quite healed.

It's at about this point where the English-built Promenade des Anglais really starts with a succession of villas, palaces, casinos, clubs and hotels.

Keep walking west and you'll see the cupola of the

(7) Palais Reine Berthe at No 11, a gorgeous Belle Epoque building constructed around 1913. It's one of the few remaining buildings of that period on the Promenade. Notice the richly decorated facade and the two sculpted ladies flanking the bow windows on the first floor.

Next up is the massive Art Deco

(8) Palais de la Méditerranée at No 13. If buildings could talk, this one would spin out quite a tale. Back in the roaring 1920s Nice was competing with other luxurious seaside resorts for the moneyed set. Looking to outdo Biarritz, Deauville and San Remo in Italy, celebrated architect Charles Dalmas was enlisted to create the mother

134

of all hotel-casinos. American philanthropist Frank Jay Gould provided the financing.

It opened in 1929 to immediate acclaim. The limestone facade was a festival of columns, arcades, sculptures and bas-reliefs. Behind it was a monumental hall and staircase, gaming rooms with towering windows, a marble atrium, a ballroom, indoor sculptures, a restaurant that could seat 2000 guests and an elaborate theater. It was the pride of the Cote d'Azur.

What happened? Bankruptcy, corruption and even murder. In 1977, Le Roux, Agnes, majority shareholder of the Palais with her mother Renée, was induced to sell her shares to Jean-Dominique Fratoni, a casino magnate with possible Mafia connections. She placed the money from the transaction in a joint account with her lover Maurice Agnelet and soon disappeared mysteriously and permanently. Both men fell under suspicion for her murder and, after many years and investigations, Agnelet was finally convicted and sent to prison.

Meanwhile, in 1978 the Palais went bankrupt after a night of possibly crooked gambling that literally "broke the bank". Fratoni sold the property to a Kuwaiti group who then sold it to a Lebanese group of financiers. Mayor Jacques Médecin, had long dreamed of turning Nice into a French Las Vegas and gave permission to demolish the building and erect a new luxury hotel complex. As Renée had gotten the facade designated a historical landmark, "only" the magnificent interior could be destroyed. The art, the stained glass windows, even the staircase were auctioned off in 1981.

After changing hands a few more times, a massive new hotel-casino was constructed behind the facade. It was inaugurated in 2004 and received its fifth star in 2009. Although undoubtedly impressive, the interior does not recall the establishment's former design in any way. The columns and bas-reliefs on the facade are gloriously intact.

The west side of the building was destroyed but the east side retains its original Art Deco features. Notice the colorful sculpture on the facade. It's by Niki de Saint Phalle (193-2002) who bequeathed a number of her works to the city of Nice.

After admiring the east side of the building, keep walking up the rue de Congrès. Turn left on the rue de France and you are on the site of the first British community in Nice, the *Faubourg de la Croix de Marbre*. Ahead is

(9) La Croix de Marbre or **Marble Cross**. Back in the 15th century a group of wealthy *Niçois* decided that what Nice needed was a congregation of Franciscan monks. They procured the land here, which was little more than a field, far from the Colline du Chateau and Vieux Nice. The monks built a friary and a church which was consecrated in 1472. The arrival of the Franciscans transformed this rustic patch of land into a neighborhood.

In 1538 Pope Paul III stayed here as part of a plan to broker a peace deal between Francis I of France and Charles V of Spain. A wobbly treaty was eventually signed by the two sovereigns who stayed in Villeneuve Loubet and Villefranche respectively. Called the *Congrès de Nice* (hence the rue de Congrès), the deal fell apart in 1543 when the French joined the Turks to lay siege to the Chateau. Although the attack was repelled the Franciscan friary was destroyed and the Franciscans eventually moved to their monastery in Cimiez. The marble cross was erected in 1568 to commemorate the Pope's visit and the misbegotten peace deal. The elegant kiosk that surrounds the cross was erected at the end of the 19th century.

Across the street is the

(10) Colonne en Marbre Blanc or **Marble Column** erected in 1823 to commemorate the passages in Nice of Pope Pius VII in 1809 and 1814. Curiously, the coat-of-arms sculpted on the pedestal is not that of the Pope but of his family, the Chiaramonti. Within it is the Croix de Lorraine which became the symbol of Free France during WWII.

The elegant mansion behind the column is the

(11) Palais Marie Christine so named in memory of the wife of King Charles-Félix. She stayed here in November 1826 shortly after its construction, and again during the winter of 1829-1830 with her husband. Widowed in 1831, she returned at the end of 1834 and then again during the winter of 1842-1843. Her initials are carved in medallions above the east and west wings. At the end of the 19th century the Anglo-American Club gathered here.

Keep going on the rue de France noting the handsome Belle Epoque buildings on the right: **Palais de la Buffa** and **Palais Alice**, both built around 1905. Turn left on rue Meyerbeer to return to the Promenade. Before continuing west, turn left to see the hotel

(12) Le Royal at No 23. Constructed in 1905 by celebrated architect Charles Dalmas (1863-1938), Le Royal is one of the few hotels on the Promenade that remains in its original state. Its style was widely imitated over the years. The main features are the flat roof topped with tiles and zinc, stucco friezes at the top of the facade and iron balconies.

Vacationing people-watchers particularly appreciated the *Terrasse des Orangiers* which allowed them to relax on a terrace shaded by orange trees and watch the passing parade. At the turn of the 20th century, the American Club gathered here.

The terrace remains a pleasant place for a drink amid orange trees and sculpture. Step inside to check out the marvelous Belle Epoque lobby with its original stuccoes and columns.

Turn back and head west. The next hotel to notice is the stately

(13) Hotel Westminster at No 27.

In 1878 a local hotelier, Victoire Schmitz, commissioned architect Castel to combine two seafront villas into one luxurious hotel. With the agreement of the Duke of Westminster, she named the hotel after him and inaugurated her property in 1881. The hotel was extensively renovated a few times since then but remains in the hands of the Schmitz and Grinda (by marriage) family.

On the ground floor behind reception don't miss the Grand Hall with turn-of-the-century Florentine frescoes. Also easily visible is the ironwork on the stairwells. If the hotel is not busy they may direct you to the paintings by François Bensa (1811-1895) depicting views of Nice prior to 1860. A beverage at the bar is excellent value if it includes a glimpse of the hotel's treasures.

Just after is the

(14) Hotel West End at No 31

which is the oldest hotel on the Promenade. Built in 1842 in a Neo-classic style, it was first the Hotel Victoria, then the Hotel de Rome before acquiring its current name in 1905.

For a total immersion in Belle Epoque, check out the gorgeous

(15) Musée Masséna next door. The museum is

located in the neoclassical Villa Masséna which was built in 1901 for Victor Masséna, grandson of Marshal Masséna. His designated architect was Hans-Georg Tersling, one of the stars of the Belle Epoque period. Victor's son bequeathed it to Nice in 1917 on the condition that the garden remain open to the public and the villa become a museum. Done! The villa slipped into decay over the years but reopened after extensive renovations in 2008.

Go through the iron gate into the luxuriant English-style garden. On your right you'll see a **memorial to the victims of Nice's 2016 terrorist attack**. On the evening of July 14, 2016 while the Promenade was full of revelers celebrating Bastille Day, a Tunisian national drove a cargo truck onto the Promenade, killing 86 people and injuring 458 others. "*En memoire de Nos Anges*" (In memory of our Angels) displays photos of the victims topped with the fountain of national tribute used in a prior commemoration. It is surmounted by a heart, formed by the names of the 86 victims, made by the football club OGC Nice.

The entrance to the museum is on the northern side past the garden. The rectangular entrance hall is an eye-popping display of classical Greek style. Notice the early 19th-century frieze of classical scenes and the statue of Napoleon Bonaparte represented as a Roman emperor. It's been welcoming visitors since the villa's opening as a reminder of the man who Marshal Masséna served. Also on the ground floor are the luxuriously outfitted reading room, dining room, portrait room, smoking room, office and Grand Salon. The friezes, moldings, inlaid wood, sculpture, chandeliers and art objects are a tribute to the19th-century taste for the ornate.

The rooms upstairs are devoted to tracing the history of Nice through portraits, drawings and paintings. There's Garibaldi in his trademark red shirt, a regal Queen Victoria, Napoleon Bonaparte and various lesser luminaries. Don't miss the representations of old Nice including a rustic Promenade des Anglais, Place Masséna, the first Anglican church in Nice, a tree-lined avenue Jean Médecin and a sleepy Port Lympia.

(open Wednesday-Monday 10am-6pm)

Across the street is the legendary

(16) Hotel Negresco, the only hotel that is as prestigious now as at its inauguration day in 1913. The Negresco was the brainchild of a Romanian immigrant, Henri Negresco, who started life as the son of an innkeeper and then found success in the hotel business. When he hired architect Edouard Niermans he insisted on catering to the tastes of his wealthy and demanding clientele. The "wow" factor was expressed in the magnificent glass roof covering an elliptical inner courtyard. The stately halls reflect an ingenious combination of neoclassical and Belle Epoque styles. And the 420 rooms were equipped with essential comforts such as anterooms and private bathrooms. Seven crowned heads of state attended the hotel's opening making it an immediate sensation.

Its luster dimmed during WWI when the hotel became a military hospital. By the end of the war, Henri Negresco found himself financially ruined. He died of cancer in 1920 and the hotel struggled to survive. In 1957 new owners took over. Paul Augier and his daughter Jeanne added to the already lavish furnishings by installing fine furniture and an exceptional collection of classical and contemporary art. The hotel was back in business.

The luminaries who stayed at the Hotel Negresco encompasses everyone from Queen Elizabeth II to the Rolling Stones—too long to list here! The sculpture outside by Niki de Saint Phalle commemorates the visit of Louis Armstrong. The hotel was named a historic monument in 1975 and maintains its allure even after the death of Jeanne Augier in 2019.

Unfortunately it's no longer possible to visit the interior unless you're a guest of the hotel, restaurant or bar. The outlandishly costumed doormen are firm. A meal at the acclaimed Chantecler restaurant would open doors and a drink in the wood-paneled bar is another way to soak up the atmosphere.

Crossing Boulevard Gambetta, there's a whole different style visible in

(17) Le Forum at No 45. Built in 1932 in response to Nice's expansion west, Art Deco master Georges Dikansky (1881-1963) created a perfectly symmetrical facade that was once topped by a clock and a barometer. The highlight was the 1400-seat cinema on the ground floor specially outfitted for the newfangled "talking films". Falling attendance caused the cinema's closure in 1982. The space is now the High Club, a fixture on Nice's nightlife scene.

Keep going another block and notice the

(18) Villa Starzynski at No 55. All that's left of this once extravagant villa are the niches and original statues on the facade. Count Starzynski, a Polish nobleman, commissioned the noted architect Sébastien Marcel Biasini (1840-1913) to build this summer residence in 1873. The interior was splendidly appointed, not least because the count was an avid art collector and a painter himself. He and his wife gave lavish costume parties and balls for the rich foreigners vacationing in Nice. The building was overhauled and two floors added in the 1930s.

Look to the right as you approach Rue Honoré Sauvan and admire the

(19) Venus Sculptures peeking out from the walls of the AC Marriott hotel. It's the work of renowned Nice artist Sacha Sosno. Part of Nice's "new realist" movement, he created these massive bronzes in 1988 for the hotel then known as the Elysée Palace.

Keep walking and you'll see a vast garden behind iron gates. It's the garden of the

(20) Villa Furtado-Heine, built between 1784 and 1787 for an Englishwoman, Penelope Rivers, aiming to give large parties for the Anglican community. At the time there was no Promenade des Anglais and the garden extended nearly to the sea. Then the Revolution happened in 1789 and the villa was seized.

During the early 19th century the villa passed from hand to bejeweled hand before landing with Madame Furtado-Heine in 1882, the wealthy widow of Hamburg banker Charles Heine. She added a floor o the top of the building and made other stylistic improvements. Preoccupied with the welfare of officers exhausted after the second French expedition to Madagascar, she donated her mansion to the Ministry of War in order to found a convalescent facility. The central pediment carries the inscription "Aux Officiers des Armées de Terre Air Mer 1895".

It's now in the hands of the Ministry of Defense and is still reserved for military officers. Known as the *Villa des Officiers*, it cannot be visited. But you can peak through the iron gates for a glimpse at the only 18th-century estate on the Promenade.

Walk on a few meters and you're in front of the red walls of the

(21) Centre Universitaire Méditerranéen

(CUM) at No 65. Although striking, the 19th-century villa is a shadow of its formal self. It was once Villa Guiglia, an ornate Belle Epoque building belonging to retired Pittsburgh iron magnate Charles Spang. His socialite daughter Rosalie made it another party-spot on the Prom until her death in 1910. She bequeathed it to the city which made it the headquarters of the prestigious Club Nautique. In 1930 writer Paul Valéry convinced mayor Jean Médecin to use it as a center for discussions and conferences on regional issues.

But fashions change and in 1935 the villa was re-done in Art Deco style. It now serves as, a place for conferences, lectures, concerts and expositions. Events take place in the glorious amphitheater. The CUM is open for visits during business hours or for special events.

Turn right on rue Paul Valéry and left on the rue de France to find the CUM stop on tramway line 2. Or perhaps, continue on to explore West Nice?

PROMENADE DES ANGLAIS MAP

Map Key

1   Neuf Lignes Obliques
2   Défly building
3   Hotel Beau Rivage
4   109 Quai des Etats-Unis
5   Chaise Bleu sculpture
6   Hotel Méridien Nice
7   Palais Reine-Berthe
8   Palais de la Méditerranée
9   La Croix en Marbre Blanc
10 Colonne en Marbre Blanc
11 Palais Marie Christine
12 Le Royal
13 Hotel Westminster
14 Hotel West End
15 Musée Masséna
16 Hotel Negresco
17 Le Forum
18 Villa Starzyinsky
19 Venus Sculptures
20 Villa Furtado-Heine
21 CUM

WEST NICE:
PARKS AND MANSIONS

Start CUM

Finish Sainte-Hélène church

Time 2 1/2 hours

Good for Getting away from crowds; Belle Epoque and Art Deco architecture; parks

Points of Interest Villa Les Palmiers, Musée d'Art Naïf, Musée des Beaux Arts

Points to Note Musée d'Art Naïf is closed Tuesday; Musée des Beaux Arts is closed Monday.

West Nice is the place to get off the beaten path, get some fresh air and visit some of Nice's lesser-known sights. Gentle hills climb north of the Promenade and become surprising rural a few kilometers inland. Until the end of the 19th century west Nice was a bucolic land of fields and farms. The wide open spaces convinced wealthy and titled foreigners to build their country estates here rather than busy Cimiez and central Nice. They hired top architects for their mansions and top landscapers to plant luxuriant gardens. Most were torn down or converted to apartment buildings after WWII but a number of modest single-family homes remain. Many are decorated with multi-colored frescoes as their owners lacked the means to install sculpted bas-reliefs. This walk covers three neighborhoods: Les Baumettes, Magnan and Fabron-Sainte Hélène stretching from east to west.

Les Baumettes is a hilly but leafy neighborhood whose name derives from the *Nissart* word *baume* or "grotto". It's unclear why as there are no grottoes here. The foot of the hill is the Baumettes plain that stretches to Castle Hill in the east.

In 1538 the plain was the scene of a meeting between Pope Paul III, Francis I of France and Charles V of Spain. As the plain was neutral territory the warring sovereigns accepted to meet here and negotiate the *Congrès de Nice* peace deal which collapsed five years later.

In the 19th century the neighborhood became a prestigious address for English, Russian, French and Americans who arrived and built vast estates. A few survive amid many single-family villas from the mid-20th century.

Magnan derives from an old French word for silk production which thrived along the Magnan river. The mighty river also powered olive mills; the Alziari company still has a mill upstream. Along its banks were vineyards, willows to be made into wicker, laundries and cardboard factories. Yet most of the neighborhood was countryside dotted with fields of carnations. In the 19th century foreigners looking for an authentic rural experience built villas here and there, to take advantage of the wild, natural beauty.

At the turn of the 20th century Greek, Armenian and Russian immigrants trickled in, starting small businesses. A long and costly project that began in 1926 and ended in 1960 covered over the Magnan river. Today it's an over-developed commercial and residential neighborhood.

Fabron-Sainte Hélène was little more than untamed woods until the 13th century when vineyards appeared and eventually fig and olive groves. But the area remained sparsely inhabited largely because of Barbary pirates. Their brutal assaults became a major problem in the 16th century and discouraged any coastal settlement.

Nor could the peasantry pray for divine protection. Getting to the churches in Old Nice involved an arduous journey across two rivers. When the Sainte Hélène church was built behind a line of coastal fortifications in the 17th century, people's safety and spiritual problems were solved.

Agriculture continued as the main activity but the area remained a rural outpost of central Nice. With the explosion of tourism in the 19th century, Fabron became attractive to wealthy visitors looking for a more countrified experience than the town center. British and Russians built extravagant villas surrounded by carefully manicured gardens. Shops and services followed and the local economy took off.

A few magnificent estates survive but most were sold to real estate developers in the 1950s and 1960s who razed the villas and erected large housing developments.

Not all was destroyed however. The old estates contained vast gardens that, in many cases, were turned into municipal parks. You'll see several picnic-perfect parks on this walk.

Start at the Centre Universitaire Méditerranéen (CUM—covered in the Promenade des Anglais walk) at No 65 Promenade des Anglais. Directly behind it is

(1) Gloria Mansions at No 123-125 rue de France.

From the concrete facade you might not guess that the building is considered a jewel of Art Deco architecture and a historic monument.

Look a little closer at that gray facade. Even better look at it in sunlight and see how it glistens. That's because the tinted concrete is encrusted with crushed oyster shells, an example of the attention to detail that characterizes this remarkable residence. Look up and see how the balconies curve like waves in the sea. Look to the top floor and notice the sculpted raptors guarding the building. They were inspired by the steel gargoyles that adorn the Chrysler Building in New York City.

The reference to New York is not accidental. The architects — Garabed Hovnanian and his brothers Barouyr and Hrant--were inspired by the apartment-hotels that populated New York at the turn of the 20th-century. Educated at Robert College in Istanbul, the Hovnanian family brought innovations such as central heating and hot water, an underground garage and built-in storefronts to their 1934 building.

But it's the design details that make Gloria Mansions a standout. Sculptor Albert Chiavacci created the Mediterranean-themed stuccoes and bas-reliefs between the balconies, over the magnificent entrance-door (usually open)

and inside the courtyard. (The Art Deco building is Gloria Mansions II on the right of the courtyard. The much earlier building to the left is clearly a Belle Epoque style.) Notice the mosaics at the end of the courtyard.

On the right is the main entrance to the building through which you can see the unique glass-mosaic created by Lasalle. For this work, the artist glued mosaics between two panes of glass.

The summit of splendor lies behind the door. Here a monumental concrete staircase supported by green-tinted columns spirals up to a glass roof. The bronze hand-crafted letter-boxes are topped with bas-reliefs depicting the many varieties of mail-delivery. The "Renseignements" sign was a classier way to indicate the presence of a concierge to receive the occasional telegram.

Although named a historical monument in 1989 the building fell into disrepair at the end of the 20th century. An extensive and scrupulous two-year renovation ended in 2015. Now this masterpiece of 20th-century architecture has been restored to its former glory as a prestigious residence.

Continue west a few steps and across the street on your right is a vast esplanade with steps leading up to the

(2) Musée des Beaux-Arts, a striking building easily visible at the top of the hill. Begun in 1878 for the Ukrainian Princess Elisabeth Kotschoubey the Neo-Renaissance style echoes the great palaces of Saint Petersburg. Construction delays sapped the stamina of the elderly princess who sold it to James Thompson, a wealthy American in 1882. The city of Nice purchased it in 1925 and transformed it into the Musée des Beaux-Arts Jules Cheret after the painter who lived and died in Nice.

The restful English garden in front is ornamented with date and palm trees and outfitted with benches. The entrance hall is eye-popping. It was designed as a party space big enough to host a 25-piece orchestra and dance floor. Under the painted 15-meter high ceiling, Nice's notables danced on a mosaic floor during sumptuous balls. Notice the lavish marble staircase. James Thompson paid 130,000 francs to build it which was the price of an entire villa at the time.

The eclectic collection displayed on two floors concentrates on artists linked to the region. The lobby and the gallery present works by Jules Cheret, Jean-Baptiste Carpeaux, Michel de Tarnowsky and the magnificent *Nymph* of Henri-Louis Cordier, in polychrome marble (1910). Notice the *Tête de vieillard* by Jean-Honoré Fragonard, Hubert Robert's *Gorges d'Ollioules* (1783) and the massive *Theseus Vanquishing the Bull at Marathon* by Carle Van Loo.

Take the staircase to the second floor and you'll immediately encounter an original plaster version of Rodin's *The Kiss (*1886)and a bronze of Carpeaux's *Génie de la Danse* (1822). Don't miss Marie Bashkirtseff's *Autoportrait a la Palette* (1884), painted shortly before she died of tuberculosis. Gustav-Adolf Mossa bequeathed a collection of his unique oils and watercolors, many of which center on his obsession with pirouettes. There's a room featuring works by Jules Cheret and another featuring Raoul Dufy's Riviera scenes. *(open Tuesday-Sunday 10am-6pm)*

Leave the museum from the back entrance on avenue des Baumettes. In front of you is avenue du Chateau de la Tour. Proceed up the street and you are in the domain of the

(3) Chateau de la Tour des Baumettes. Now

a private residence, the crenelated tower of the main

building rises ahead on the right. It looks medieval but in fact it was built in 1860 by Audiffret, a prosperous local merchant enamored of Neo-Gothic style. Russian architect Louis Dunski created the pastiche which later owners embellished. It was divided into individual lots in 1922.

Go back downhill to the Promenade des Anglais and turn right. Notice

(4) Les Loggias at No 87, a remarkable work by Georges Dikansky (1881-1963), the Russian emigré that created some of Nice's most iconic buildings. Built in 1947, the continuous balconies of the top five floors were an innovation at the time. Even more striking is the ornamental ironwork of the balconies. Combining flat bars and thin bars in intersecting patterns creates a delightfully lacy effect.

Continue walking and you'll come to the

(5) Palais de l'Agriculture which was built to house the *Societe d'Agriculture et Horticulture* (Agriculture and Gardening Association. Inaugurated in 1901, this handsome yellow Belle Epoque structure is proof that you don't need an architect to make a building. The secretary of the Agricultural Society who was also an engineer, Paul Martin, came up with the building plans. The idea behind the Agricultural Society was to improve the sorry state of Nice agriculture through courses and workshops. The project was considered so important to the economic development of the city that French President Emile Loubet attended the opening ceremony.

A major facelift in 2009 restored the building to its former glory although some grumbled that the color was too bright. "It will fade" said the city. The Society is still going strong and there's no problem popping into the interior during business hours.

Notice the **Flower Pot Sculptures** on the side. Artist Jean-Pierre Raynaud created the two-pot *Metamorphose* to give a mystical dimension to the common flower pot.

You're walking over the Magnan river which still flows directly into the Baie des Anges at this point.

Continue up the north side of the Promenade and you cannot miss the

(6) Villa Collin-Huovila at No 139, perhaps the

most eccentric building on the Promenade. This rare (for Nice) Art Nouveau festival of caryatids, polychrome ceramics and gaily painted masonry is topped by a red "samurai helmet" as a roof.

Architect Marius Allinges designed it as a single-family dwelling for Collin d'Huovila who made his fortune patenting a multiple air chamber system for car tires. A sculpture by François Virieux that adorns the southeast corner depicts a caryatid receiving roses from cherubs. In 1919 it became the property of local aviator Auguste Maïcon and is now available for short-term vacation rentals.

Next to it at No 137 is the **Villa Monada** which is a modern Art Deco refurbishment of a Belle Epoque villa. The sparse lines are an odd contrast to its flamboyant neighbor.

Continue up the Promenade and you'll come to a giant blue building which is the

(7) Fondation Lenval, Nice's foremost children's hospital. This glittering building was finished in 1999 and replaced a 19th-century children's hospital. In 2008 actress Angelina Jolie chose to deliver her twins here, making Lenval briefly the center of an international media storm.

Just across the rue Lenval is

(8) La Couronne, at No 167. This stately Art Deco building was also built in 1926 by Georges Dikansky. He hired his favorite ceramists, Gentil & Bourdet, to decorate the top floor as well as the small detached villa in front of the main building. The spacious garden in front of the building separates it from street noise.

Continue west a few blocks and turn right at the Art Deco **La Mascotte** (1930s) heading up avenue de Fabron. On avenue de la Californie turn left and in about 10 meters you'll come to a working

(9) Fountain installed in 1890. The inscription is in *Nissart*, the local dialect: *Dounas a beure en aquelu ch'an set*, which means "Let drink those who are thirsty". The water is perfectly fine to drink.

Return to the corner and turn left to continue up avenue de Fabron as it curves to the left. On your left you'll see the vast **Grands Cédres** residence. Keep following avenue de Fabron and on your right is another modern residence, **Chateau Sainte Anne**, that was once a vast estate containing two splendid villas: *L'Hermitage* (1920) and *L'Africaine* (1896). The estate was demolished in 1984 and turned into a residential development.

154

Continue up avenue de Fabron until the sign "Archives Municipales". Go through the gate to Grand Cédres on the left and keep going up through the parking lot until you come to the most remarkable estate in west Nice, the

(10) Villa Les Palmiers or Palais du Marbre.

Its story begins in 1795 when a clever but unscrupulous businessman, Andre Gastaud exploited the confusion and corruption of the Revolutionary period to buy a huge tract of land in Fabron. In 1840 the property passed to his grand-nephew, Honoré. On it he built a luxurious residence for himself, several "guest cottages", farmhouses, an olive oil mill, gardens and groves.

In 1860 he received Napoleon III and his wife, Eugenie but his glory was fleeting. 10 years later the Franco-Prussian war left Gastaud in financial ruin. He put his estate up for sale and sold it to an English art dealer, Ernest Gambart, who renamed it *Les Palmiers.*

Gambart hired the go-to architect of the era, Sébastien Marcel Biasini, to transform the principal residence. Biasini chose a Neo-palladian style, modeled on Chatsworth House in Derbyshire, to create a Marble Palace. Twenty-seven boats sailed from Carrara, Italy laden with marble for the statues, columns, balustrades, walls and floors. The lavish rooms became a showcase for his immense art collection and a place to receive famous friends such as Rosa Bonheur and Sarah Bernhardt.

The owners that succeeded Gambart couldn't help putting their own imprint on the property. Baron Falz-Fein dug an artificial pond in the English-style garden. Argentinian meat-baron Edouard Soulas renovated the interior in a neoclassical Louis XV style replete with chinoiserie, paneling, inlaid wood and gilt. He also constructed a French garden around the pond and a false rock garden at its southern edge.

Later the villa was used as a movie set. *Lola Montes* by Max Ophuls, *Cela s'appelle l'aurore* by Luis Buñuel, *Foreign Intrigue* with Robert Mitchum were filmed here.

It was the end of an era in 1961 when the city granted permission to demolish everything except Les Palmiers and its garden. In its place arose the towering *Grands Cédres* apartment buildings and the *Voie Rapide* roadway. Currently the Marble Palace houses the Municipal Archives and is only open for visits during the temporary historical exhibitions that take place regularly between March and September.

The splendid garden with the pond and statuary is open to the public and free to stroll. Ignore the drab official entrance to the municipal archives on the north and go around to the southern side to admire the marble facade and classical statuary. Statues on the first floor niches represent Poetry, Music, Dance and Astronomy. The rooftop statues represent Architecture, Painting, Sculpture and Drawing. Over the loggia an engraving reminds you that "A thing of beauty is a joy forever". Or so said poet John Keats. The rooftop terrace was used for parties and welcomed tsarina Maria Alexandrovna in 1858.

Stroll the path to the right of the garden which displays the villa's original classical statuary and columns in a lovely, shady setting. Don't miss the ornate **dovecote** on the southern end.

Leave the estate through the same gate in which you arrived and keep going uphill. Across the road on your right is the

(11) Parc Indochine, a restful neighborhood park that commemorates the French presence in Indochine (1887-1954). The park is on land that originally belonged to the Chateau Sainte Anne. Landscape designer Octave Godard (1877-1958) had planted a forest of palm trees around the villa *L'Africaine*, reflecting a contemporary taste for exoticism.

The authorization to demolish the chateau in 1984 was expressly conditioned on the creation of a municipal park. And so it was done. The forest of palm trees was tamed into a sedate palm tree lined walkway.

Chateau Sainte Anne

Keep climbing the hill and you'll come to a small roundabout. Straight ahead is the entrance to the

(12) Parc Carol De Roumanie, another delightful municipal park that was once part of an estate. In this case, the park is the last remnant of the **Chateau de Fabron**. Built in 1870 on the property of Honoré Gastaud (him again), the chateau was then sold to Ernest II, the German Duke of Saxe-Cobourg. Sometimes nicknamed "Ernest the Depraved" for his incessant womanizing, the lascivious duke managed to confine his interests to food, music and theater during his regular stays in Nice.

The Saxe-Cobourg family held onto the property until 1930 when they sold it to King Carol of Romania. After a years-long legal struggle the city of Nice acquired the property in 1956, tore down the royal residence and created this park. Stretching 2.3 hectares, the park hosts a children's playground, miniature golf course and a snack stand.

Next to the entrance is an **old farmhouse** dating from 1873 that is the only remaining structure from the original Chateau de Fabron estate.

To the left is the entrance to the

(13) Musée International d'Art Naïf lodged in

the former Chateau Sainte Hélène. The art museum lies behind a forbidding iron gate in the midst of a sprawling park strewn with sculptures. We're still in Gastaud-land here. The estate was once part of the same parcel of land that Honoré Gastaud inherited in 1840. Gastaud erected the Chateau Sainte Hélène and various annexes.

When Gastaud's life fell apart in 1870, the man who created the Monte Carlo Casino, Francois Blanc, bought the terrain and named it the Villa Blanc. In 1904 the American Henry Welchman Bartol bought it and hired Nice architect Aaron Messiah (1858-1940) to transform the old Chateau. Messiah was a popular choice among the local Anglophone population as he spoke English fluently in addition to his undeniable artistic talent. His transformation of the chateau was so complete that little remains of the original style.

Upon Bartol's death in 1923, perfumer François Coty bought the property. It passed to his wife Yvonne upon their divorce in 1930. The building was again remodeled and in 1973 the city of Nice took over and used it to house the naïve art collection of Anatole Jakovsky.

The museum is a fun and "un-museumy" place to visit. Naïve art favors the spontaneity of an individual vision where each visitor is invited into an imaginary journey. Although the pictorial ideas are simple they have a whimsical allure.

Paintings, sculptures, drawings and posters trace the evolution of this art form through the works of its most famous painters: Bauchant, Bombois, Vivin, Séraphine, Rimbert, Lefranc, Rabuzin, Ivan and Josip Généralic, Lackovic, Grandma Moses, O 'Brady, Haddelsey, Ligabue, Vivancos, Douanier Rousseau and more.

A donation from the National Museum of Modern Art, Center Georges Pompidou further enriches this ensemble with works by Bombois, Bauchant, Vivin, Séraphine and Rimbet. *(Open 10am-12:30pm. and 1:30 -6pm Wednesday-Monday)*

After leaving the museum, turn left onto avenue Val Marie. You'll quickly come to the

(14) Chateau Barla at 28 avenue Val Marie. You'll recognize it easily because the wrought iron entrance gate spells out the name. This chateau was also part of the original Gastaud estate and where Ernest Gambart stayed while Les Palmiers was being rebuilt.

Gambart sold it to Englishman George Bishop and his wife, Penelope in 1873 who used their magnificent residence to showcase artists, musicians and composers. The concerts and garden parties wound down after George Bishop died in 1883 but Penelope stayed on until WWI, becoming a generous local philanthropist. Although the Neo-Gothic elements have been stripped, you can get a glimpse of the square crenelated watchtower from the gate. It's a private residence now.

Head downhill on avenue Val Marie, a leafy street with a number of beautiful villas, and you'll come to a tiny roundabout across from the residence La Louvière. Cross it and go down the stairs. Turn right and you'll come to the

(15) Leliwa de Rohozinski Manor with its distinctive array of turrets and an even more striking square watchtower.

In the late 1880s a Polish count, Michel Leliwa de Rohozinsky, bought the terrain and hired Polish architect Adam Dettloff to create this fantastical pastiche of medieval styles. The impressive entrance hall had a monumental stairway in wood sculpted by Italian artisans. The count was a personal friend of Prince Louis Napoleon and an enthusiastic fan of the Bonaparte family. He filled rooms with letters, books and memorabilia of Napoleon and had the architect install a bust of his idol on the eastern facade of his castle where it remains. Look for the imperial eagles at the four-corners of the turret.

The manor is now used for offices. The interior is off-limits but it's easy to admire the unusual exterior.

160

Continue downhill to the avenue de la Californie. Straight ahead on the right at No 195 is the striking

(16) Villa La Luna.

Built in 1915, it was the last Belle Epoque building on the Promenade. It had been allowed to fall into ruin since the 1980s but the city finally wrested control back from its Kuwaiti owner, restored it and reopened it to the public in 2020. It now houses the Maison des Associations. It's possible to pop inside for a peek during business hours. The interior highlight is the marble staircase with a wrought-iron railing.

Turn left and head east. Walk past the Radisson Blu hotel to the

(17) Square Felix Ziem.

This peaceful park was the site of the **Pauline battery** built by French revolutionary forces in the 18th century when the Fabron coast was a military zone, largely because of several devastating raids by Barbary pirates. The belt of fortifications that protected the neighborhood lasted until 1894 when the battery was dismantled.

Turn inland and just behind the park is the

(18) Eglise Sainte-Hélène

at No 142 avenue de Californie. The austere yellow facade is plain but the church was essential to the development of the neighborhood. The first chapel was erected here in 1650 by the wealthy Rossignoli family to cater to local farmers cultivating the land. As it wasn't a parish, the sacraments couldn't be performed here though. At last in 1728 the Bishop of Nice ordered the construction of Sainte Hélène, the first parish church created outside the city walls. The church was rebuilt in the 19th century and is now a historic monument.

You are now midway between the Fabron and Sainte Hélène stops on tramway line 2.

Gloria Mansions

WEST NICE MAP

Map Key

1   Gloria Mansions

2   Musée des Beaux-Arts de Nice

3   Chateau de la Tour des Baumettes

4   Les Loggias

5   Palais de l'Agriculture

6   Villa Collin-Huovila

7   Lenval Children's Hospital

8   La Couronne

9   Fountain

10   Villa Les Palmiers--Palais du Marbre

11   Parc de l'Indochine

12   Parc Carol De Roumanie

13   Musée International d'Art Naïf

14   Chateau Barla

15   Leliwa de Rohozinski Manor

16   Villa La Luna

17   Square Félix Ziem

18   Eglise Sainte Helene

PROMENADE DU PAILLON: FOLLOWING THE RIVER

Start Monument du Centenaire

Finish Place Garibaldi

Time 2 hours

Good for Kids, gardens, parks, contemporary art

Points of Interest Jardin Albert 1er, Coulée Verte, Place Garibaldi, MAMAC (Museum of Modern and Contemporary Art)

Points to Note MAMAC is closed on Monday.

Once upon a time, a river ran through it. The Paillon river divided old Nice from new Nice until 1868 when the first covering was built. Gone were the washerwomen beating their laundry along its banks but also gone were the devastating floods that swept through the old town every few decades when the river overflowed its banks. To warn the population of an imminent flood men once galloped through the streets on horseback shouting "Paioun ven! Paioun ven!" (The Paillon is coming!)

A series of drab, 20th-century structures on top of the covered river were demolished in 2011 and replaced by the marvelous Promenade du Paillon. Also known as the *coulee verte* or "greenway", this 40,000 sq meter promenade is simultaneously a sculpture park, botanical garden, and innovative playground. From the magnificent water mirror to the marine animals in the children's playground, there are constant reminders of the water flowing underneath. It's an extraordinary green oasis that's pleasant to stroll through or hang out for a while with or without kids. The park is well-equipped with chairs, drinking fountains and public toilets.

Start at the soaring

(1) Monument du Centenaire de la Réunion à la France built in 1896 to honor the 100th anniversary of Nice's vote to join France.

But Nice officially opted in to France in 1860 so how could this be the 100th anniversary? Because the question was first put to Nice in a 1792 referendum. There was an overwhelming "yes" vote and the Revolutionary Convention proclaimed the integration in 1793. But it was not a free and fair election. The vote was conducted under the watchful eyes of French Revolutionary forces and not every town was asked to participate. Hence the "re-vote" in 1860.

When the statue was commissioned in 1892, the idea was to solidify Nice's place in the French Republic since a segment of the native Italian population was still adjusting to the new management. Designed by Jules Febvre and sculpted by Joseph Allar (1845-1925), everything about the monument was intended to reinforce the message of French Nice. The bronze Winged Victory (*Niké*) on the top alludes to Nice's founding as the Greek city of Nikaïa. The marble base of the obelisk shows Nice as a young woman embracing France, an older woman who is leaning on a beam symbolizing the Republic. The composition is intended to be calm, maternal and reassuring. On the opposite side is a sculpture of a nude who represents the Mediterranean. She is surmounted by the coat-of-arms of Nice topped by a crown. Inscriptions on either side give more details about the commemorative events and its inauguration in 1896..

Behind the statue is the

(1) Jardin Albert 1er, one of Nice's oldest public

parks. It extends from Place Masséna to the Promenade des Anglais and was built over the mouth of the Paillon river. The park is structured to flow like a river with the widest part opening onto the Promenade des Anglais. The river is still visible across the Promenade as it empties into Centenaire beach.

From the beginning of the 19th century it was clear that the aristocrats trickling down to Nice needed a shady, verdant space to take a stroll and enjoy Nice's healthy air. The idea of a public garden was becoming popular in

Europe and there happened to be the perfect space along the banks of the Paillon river. The city drew up the basic plan in 1835 along with the species of plants and trees to adorn the space. Local engineer Joseph Duranty was entrusted with the design and the first park opened in 1852. It was an immediate hit with locals and visitors who loved the pine, cypress and olive trees interspersed with Oriental and African vegetation. The choice of vegetation was part of Nice's marketing plan as an "exotic" destination.

That relatively small park is now the **Jardin de l'Armenie**, lying west of the Jardin Albert 1er across the avenue de Verdun. In 1864 the river was dammed at its mouth to construct a bridge, expanding the park. In 1895 the river was covered from Place Masséna to the sea which allowed the park to expand further and take the form we see today.

The park cycled through a variety of names before finally settling on Albert 1er in a tribute to the Belgian king who heroically resisted the Germans in WWI. The WWII years saw considerable damage to the park after the German occupiers erected numerous blockhouses. In 1945 the park was redesigned and the

(2) Theatre de Verdure was built on the site of an artificial cave. This immensely popular open-air concert space lies behind the statue and is separated by fencing. It hosts the Nice Jazz Festival each July and presents a diverse program of concerts the rest of the year. The theater is adorned with **statues of Venus and Apollo** created in 1946 by sculptor Alfred Janniot.

Enter the park through the gate to the left of the statue. On your left is a

(3) Bandstand built in 1868.

Take the ramp on the right and you'll come to the

(4) Fontaine des Trois Graces by Antoniucci
Volti. The three Greek goddesses grouped in the center of
the fountain are Euphrosyne, Aglae and Thalia. Despite the
classical motif, the work only dates from the late 1960s.

Follow the same path to the **Bust of Albert 1er**. Ahead
is Bernar Venet's massive

(5) Arc 115.5° an iconic sculpture that represents the
curvature of the Baie des Anges. Bernar Venet is a renowned
conceptual artist, born in 1941 and with a studio in Nice.
The statue was inaugurated in 1988 to commemorate the
100th anniversary of the "Côte d'Azur". Previously known as
the "Riviera", French writer Stephen Liegeard was the first
to refer to the "Azur Coast" in his book, *Côte d'Azur*,
published in 1888.

Turn right at the bust and follow the path south to see
the

(6) Fontaine des Phocéens also known as
Fontaine des Tritons. Triton was a Greek god and tritons
came to mean mermen to the Greeks. In this composition,
the tritons support a basin with jets emerging from conchs
and large shells. The exact provenance of these white marble
statues is unclear but somehow they wound up in the
possession of the powerful Lascaris family, supposedly as
the result of an excavation in Greece. In 1830 Consul Arson,

a local official, had the triton statues arranged into a fountain and placed it in front of the old Augustine Convent (now the site of the Lycée Masséna) to commemorate a new pipeline that brought water to central Nice. The fountain was later moved to the place des Phocéens (now the Jardin Albert 1er) as it was more convenient for the locals to access. In 1940 the fountain was moved to the Villa Paradiso in Cimiez for protection during the war and eventually returned to its current location.

Follow the path a few steps more and on the right is the 1869 bronze

(7) Lioness Statue by Clovis Masson (1838-1913). Locals claim that the large hole in the lioness's posterior was drilled by Germans during the occupation, perhaps to see if there were precious metals inside.

Circle round to the left passing the traditional **carousel** and head north. Just before the park's exit is the

(8) Plateau des Brumes or Plateau of Mists where clouds of mist rise from hundreds of fog machines under a stone surface of 1400 sq meters. The effect is mystical and it's a great place to cool off on a hot day. Unfortunately, the space is often used for other purposes in the off-season. Leaving the park, turn left to arrive at the

(9) Place Masséna, the heart and soul of Nice as well as its geographic center. Forming a link between the Vieille Ville and the wide boulevard Jean-Médecin, Place Masséna is where *Niçois* gather for any important event. From open-air concerts to a Sunday stroll, it's an extraordinarily convivial spot with statues, fountains, benches and sculpture.

Place Masséna is also the center of festivities during Nice's Carnival, a yearly event that begins in February sometime before Fat Tuesday and ends sometime after. The Carnival tradition dates at least from the 13th century and includes parades, floats and the famous *Bataille des Fleurs* in which locals on flower-bedecked floats toss flowers at the spectators. As elsewhere in Europe, the Carnival provided an opportunity for the oppressed peasant class to mock the aristocracy. The masks and disguises protected them from repercussions for what would ordinarily be a beheading offense. It's now the highlight of Nice's winter season, drawing tens of thousands of visitors from across France and Europe.

The northern part of the Place Masséna was constructed from 1832 to 1850 after plans to put a church here fell through. The architect, Joseph Vernier, modeled the Italianate arcades that fringe the square on the Rue Rivoli in

Paris but the colors—red walls and green windows—echo Ligurian style. It was dedicated to Marshal Andre Masséna in 1852. The south side of the square was built when this part of the Paillon river was covered over.

The *Fontaine du Soleil* in the center of the square, contains five bronze statues based on Greek mythology representing Earth, Mars, Venus, Saturn and Mercury. They surround a 7-ton statue of a nude Apollo. Inaugurated in 1956, Apollo's nudity scandalized right-thinking *Niçois*. Apart from the nudity the sheer size of the god's endowments caused outrage. The sculptor, Alfred Janniot (1889-1969) was summoned to chisel down the offending protrusion. That did nothing to calm sensibilities and the statue was repeatedly vandalized before being exiled to Nice's former football stadium far away from central Nice.

The other statues and the fountain steadily deteriorated and were removed in 1990, to be replaced by an unimpressive mound. With the arrival of the tramway in 2007 the statues and fountains were repaired and reinstalled and, at last, in 2011 Apollo in all his glory made a triumphant return.

The tramway also prompted a complete redesign of Place Masséna. Vehicles were banned, benches arrived and the towering **sculptures** of the Catalan artist, Jaume Plensa, arose to punctuate the square. Named "Conversation in Nice", these seven statues represent the continents and are brilliantly illuminated at night.

Pass through the gate on the eastern side of Place Masséna to enter the "**coulee verte**" and you'll immediately come to the

(10) Miroir d'eau or **Water Mirror.** Undoubtedly the star attraction of the park, this delightful installation is a shallow (2cm high) reflecting pond with 128 water jets that periodically erupt and bubble down. At night the jets are illuminated and on hot summer days kids run through it shrieking with joy.

On either side of the Water Mirror are plants and trees from South America. Note the Jubea spectabilis or Chilean coconut tree that produces small, edible fruit.

Just after the Water Mirror on the south side is the

(11) Nikaïa Sculpture the Greek goddess of victory. When the Greeks conquered the Ligurians in 350BC, they named their new city, Nikaïa which became Nicaea in Latin and Nice in French. Local artist Cyril de la Patellière created this statue in 2019.

Continue through the park, cross the street and you'll be in front of the

(12) Masséna Statue. After the Annexation of 1860, Nice was anxious to cement the city's ties to France, particularly since many citizens of Italian descent were against the Empire and preferred to rally around Garibaldi. As a French patriot, proud of his Nice origins, Masséna was the perfect hero.

This 7 meter high statue was designed by Albert Ernest Carrier-Belleuse (1824-1887) and inaugurated on 15 August 1869, Napoleon's birthday. The statue represents the general at the Battle of Essling, as he sends a reply to Napoleon. The bas-reliefs on the plinth, also in bronze, represent the Battle of Zurich, the surrender of Genoa, and an allegorical figure, Glory, who is writing Masséna's name on the pediment of history.

The gardens in this part of the park display foliage from Australia and New Zealand. In addition to the eucalyptus trees, there are immense ferns and a giant ficus.

Continue walking, cross the street and you'll come to the

(13) Children's Playground which is unique

enough that adults also will find it worth a peek. In addition to newly installed trampolines there are wooden sculptures of marine animals that children can crawl through and play in. For toddlers there's a tortoise; slightly older kids can play in the two dolphins or the giant whale equipped with multiple ropes, nets, bars, rings and a slide.

The vegetation in this part of the park comes from Africa.

Parallel to the north side of the park and across the avenue Félix Faure is the

(14) Lycée Masséna, a prestigious high school that is

also a historical monument as the site has been devoted to education for nearly 400 years. First it was an Augustinian friary built in 1623. Then it became a "central school" under the Revolution. In 1803 work began to transform it into an "imperial high school" which finally opened its doors in 1812. It became a "Collegio Convitto Nazionale" in 1848. It was here that the electors were called to vote for the reunification of Nice with France on April 15, 1860. It later became an "imperial" high school, then a "national" high school.

175

In 1909 the architect Henri Ebrard designed the new building in Art Nouveau style with balconies, terraces, galleries and mosaics. Interrupted by WWI, the building wasn't finished until 1931. The clock tower is the symbol of the school. Underneath the clock tower is a sundial inscribed with the motto of the school "Horas ne numerem nisi serenas" (I wish to count only the happy hours).

The list of famous graduates include the writers Romain Gary, Apollinaire, Louis Nucéra, Max Gallo and Joseph Kessel. Painter Yves Klein, scientist Paul Montel and aviator Roland Garros were also among the many famous graduates.

19th-century view of Lycée Masséna and the Pont Vieux

The paved north-south path that cuts through the Promenade in front of the Lycée was once the site of a 13th century stone bridge over the Paillon river. It was named the Pont Saint Antoine until the beginning of the 19th century when it acquired the name Pont Vieux to distinguish it from the Pont Neuf that had just been built near Place Masséna. For nearly six centuries it was the only bridge over the Paillon river.

Return to the park and continue to the last monument the

(15) Statue of Michelangelo's David. Created
by the Tesconi art foundry in Pietrasanta in 1995, this bronze reproduction of the Renaissance masterpiece makes a fitting end to the Promenade that began with the nude Apollo on the Place Masséna.

Leave the park after the statue. Turn left to visit the

(16) Eglise Saint Jean Baptiste-Le Voeu, also
known as the **Eglise Notre Dame des Grâces,**
a handsome neoclassical church at the end of a carefully manicured little park. Like so many Nice churches, *Eglise Le Voeu* was built in response to a cholera epidemic. It was the early 1830s and the disease was sweeping the region wreaking devastation in its wake. In six months there were 100,000 deaths in France. On April 15, 1832 the city council, in a special session, made a solemn vow (*voeu*): if Nice was spared the epidemic, the city would place itself under the protection of the Virgin and build a new church. Also, the city would organize a ceremony each year to renew its commitment to the Virgin.

Nice escaped the epidemic without a single death. Was it the Virgin or the strict quarantine that separated Nice from the lands west of the Var river? Locals were sure it was the

Virgin and planning for the new church began a few years later.

The first site was supposed to be on Place Masséna but the propensity of the Paillon river to flood encouraged planners to look elsewhere. Also this was an empty space with no troublesome houses to expropriate. Construction began in 1841, supervised by the Italian architect Charles Mosca and finished eleven years later. Promise kept!

The promise to renew the vow each year has also been kept during the annual *Fête de Voeu*. In late May or early June, the Mayor leads a procession through Vieux Nice and again pronounces the vow to the Virgin on Place Saint-François. It's followed by a ceremony in this church.

With its columned portico and classical symmetry, the church's Palladian style is reminiscent of Turin. No surprise as Nice was part of Turin-based Savoy at the time. Notice the coat-of-arms of Nice on the pediment and the sculpted figures on top which represent Religion.

The interior is styled simply and can look under-decorated by the standards of Nice's lavish baroque churches. Notice the altar painting depicting Saint Nicolas de Tolentino meditating. This saint was reputed to protect the sick. Most interesting is the altar painting representing *Le voeu de Nice*. Swiss painter Edouard-Caspar Hauser (1807-1864) shows the Virgin protecting Nice surrounded by importuning young ladies who were probably part of the local nobility. At the bottom is a view of Nice.

The chapel dedicated to the Virgin (*La Madone des Graces*) echoes the altar painting in a sculpted group showing the Virgin and two angels. At her feet are the coat-of-arms of Nice and surrounding the niche are allegories of Faith, Hope and Charity. The statue of the Virgin is removed each year to join the *Fête de Voeu* procession.

Retrace your steps crossing the Traverse de la Bourgada to boulevard Jean Jaurés. To the left is Place Jacques Toja and the

(17) Crypte Archeologique. The "crypt" is a 2000 sq meter archaeological site that was excavated with the construction of tram line 1. All that's visible above ground is a glass tower with a staircase but underneath are the remains of Nice's fortifications that were destroyed in 1706. The site can be visited by appointment only through the Centre du Patrimoine and tours are in French but it's well worth it. For now, know that you're standing more or less on top of the Bastion Saint Sébastien which protected the Porte Pairolière a little further on. This was the northernmost limit of Vieux Nice.

Across the street is the Promenade des Arts and the

(18) Théatre National de Nice which is the center of Nice's theatrical scene. Take the steps up to the sculpture terrace for a look at the *Stabile* by Calder, *Man with a Suitcase* by Borovsky and *Loch Ness Monster* by Niki de Saint Phalle.

Now in the mood for art? You're in the right place. At the foot of the stairs is the entrance to

(19) MAMAC (Museum of Modern and Contemporary Art), Nice's largest and most prestigious art museum. Focusing on art from 1960 onward, the museum is an excellent place to explore the works of Yves Klein, Arman, Ben, César, Martial Raysse and Niki de

Saint Phalle. Known as the *Ecole de Nice,* these innovative Nice-based artists drew inspiration from Pop Art, New Realism, Fluxus and Supports/Surfaces. Works by Warhol, Lichtenstein, Frank Stella and Ellsworth Kelly are included for comparison. Show up at 4pm Saturday (daily in July and August) and get a guided tour (€6) in English of the museum. And don't miss the rooftop terrace with its sweeping views of Nice.

(open Tuesday-Sunday 11am-6pm)

Across from MAMAC is

(20) Place Garibaldi, the oldest and liveliest of Nice's large squares, designed in 1782 by the architect Antoine Spinelli (1726-1819) It also may be the most beautiful square with its circle of arcaded baroque buildings around a statue of Nice-born hero Guiseppe Garibaldi. A recent renovation has restored the original trompe l'oeil windows and shutters.

When Spinelli began the project, the square was a large open space still filled with rubble from Louis XIV's destruction of the Chateau in 1706. The idea was to create a grandiose square to welcome the Savoy dukes on their voyages from Turin. He chose to model the square after the Piazza Vittorio in Turin, which must have made the dukes feel as though they never left home..

Spinelli's plans for a grand square that could host festivals, military parades and mass gatherings were complicated by the fact that the space contained a popular church, *Notre Dame du Sincaire.* Dedicated to the Virgin who supposedly appeared there during the siege of 1543, the church had been the site of an annual pilgrimage. The church got in the way of the construction project though so, goodbye church.

180

Instead, Spinelli built a new church, the **Chapelle du Saint-Sépulcre de Nice**, which the Blue Penitents purchased in 1784. In a nod to the older church, three Turkish cannonballs from the 1543 siege are mounted on the facade. To the right of the door is the consecration plaque of the older church that recounts the events of 1543. Some of the stones from the old church were used in building the pillars.

Behind the entrance a staircase leads to the chapel which contains treasures from the Blue Penitents' former church. Nice painter Emmanuel Costa decorated the ceilings in the late 19th century. Other artworks include the *Assumption of the Virgin* by Louis-Abraham van Loo, Christ emerging from the tomb, and a cycle of 17th and 18th-century paintings showing the devotions of the Blue Penitent brotherhood.

The square had a succession of names reflecting the politics of the time. It was first known as Piazza Vittoria, then Place Victoire (1792), Place République (1793), Place Napoléon (1806), Place Victor (1714), Place Napoléon (1860), Place République (1870) and then finally Place Garibaldi in 1871 in honor of the *Niçois* hero.

The center of the square is a fountain with **a statue of Garibaldi.** The Garibaldi statue was designed by Antoine Etex and Gustav Deloye and erected in 1891 to honor the much celebrated hero, Giuseppe Maria Garibaldi (1807-1882). Garibaldi was born in Nice to a seafaring family and fought passionately for Italian unification which he helped bring about. He supported liberation movements around the globe including in Brazil, Uruguay and the United States on the side of the Union. He was anti-papal and for women's liberation. What he did not support was France's annexation of Nice under the Treaty of Turin in 1860. Despite his ferocious opposition to his hometown becoming a French city, he later fought for France in the Franco-Prussian war of 1870.

With a clenched fist, the general is clad in his famous red shirt and facing Italy. His back is to the church which is appropriate given his anti-clericalism. Under the statue is a bronze plaque that represents France and Italy watching over a cradle (France). Look for the rooster that symbolizes France and the wolf that represents Italy. The two bronze lions represent Garibaldi's sons, Menotti and Riciotti. The base appears to emerge from prows which recall Garibaldi's seafaring origins. In the center of each side of the base is a medallion with the coat-of-arms of Nice.

Try to catch the **handicrafts market** the first Sunday of every month that showcases the work of local artisans.

Place Garibaldi is a great place to grab a bite to eat in one of the outdoor cafes. Open long hours and serving all day, *Cafe de la Place* and *Giuseppe and Pepino* are popular choices. Or, opt for a more traditional dining experience at *Cafe de Turin,* known for its seafood.

Jardin Albert 1er 19th century

PROMENADE DU PAILLON MAP

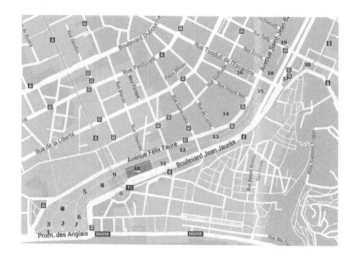

Map Key

1   Monument du Centenaire

2   Théatre de Verdure de Nice

3   Bandstand

4   Fountain des Trois Graces

5   Arc de 115.5°

6   Fontaine des Phocéens

7   Lioness statue

8   Plateau des Brumes

9   Place Masséna

10   Miroir d'eau

11   Nikaïa Sculpture

12   Masséna Statue

13   Children's Playground

14   Lycée Masséna

15   David Statue

16   Église Saint Jean-Baptiste – le Voeu

17   Crypte Archeologique

18   Théatre National de Nice

19   MAMAC

20   Place Garibaldi

QUARTIER DES MUSICIENS

Start Jardin Alsace-Lorraine

Finish Gare Thiers

Time 2 hours

Good for Belle Epoque and Art Deco architecture, Jewish history

Points of Interest: La Rotonde, La Pergola, Palais Baréty, Hotel Oasis, Hotel Excelsior, Palais Meyerbeer, Post Office

The Quartier des Musiciens is one of Nice's most elegant and prestigious neighborhoods. Bordered on the north by the train station and the south by boulevard Victor Hugo, these wide streets stretch from boulevard Gambetta in the west to avenue Jean Médecin in the east. As the neighborhood was designed to house the moneyed set, architects outdid themselves in creating beautiful buildings. Walking the streets is like touring a living museum of architectural style.

HISTORY

Before Nice's first train rolled into the station in 1864, there was nothing here but a fertile plain that furnished local markets with fruits, vegetables and flowers. It was peaceful and the air was fresh. Winter visitors staying in other neighborhoods made their way here for a refreshing stroll in the country.

The idea of putting a train station here in the middle of nowhere initially provoked ridicule. But the mayor who planned it, François Malausséna, knew something the public didn't. Nice's urban planning commission, the Consiglio d' Ornato had already decided that this part of the countryside was to be developed into a prestigious neighborhood for wealthy foreigners.

Even before the train station opened, Nice architect François Aune got to work laying out streets in a grid pattern. Boulevard Victor Hugo was the first. Later the streets were named after the composers whose works were frequently presented in Nice: Rossini, Meyerbeer, Gounod, Berlioz, Verdi. With a convenient train link to Paris it wasn't long before Russians and British, followed by rich Americans arrived. Some built mansions along the wide boulevards.

Others stayed in luxurious new hotels. They financed the construction of churches which satisfied social as well as spiritual needs.

From the late 19th-century to the onset of WWI, the predominant style was Belle Epoque. The elaborate ornamentation, stuccoes, friezes, cupolas and decorative details scream money and make the style easy to recognize. If the building vaguely resembles a birthday cake, it's Belle Epoque. In the interwar period in the 1920s and 193s, Art Deco became popular with the bourgeoisie that was settling the neighborhood. Here the style is more geometrical but jazzed up with mosaics, bas-reliefs and ironwork.

Many of the mansions were named palais. Why be humble? In fact the word "palais" simply denotes a building designed for residential use. During the Belle Epoque period, the palais were occupied by individual families but later buildings were intended as multi-family dwellings. On this walk, you'll see stunning examples of each style interspersed with more modern buildings that fit into a harmonious urban landscape.

Not all of the hotels have happy stories. You'll see one with a truly sordid history dating from WWII, when it was used by the Nazis to deport the local Jewish population.

Start at the

(1) Jardin Alsace-Lorraine next to the Alsace Lorraine tram stop. Created in 1885 just as the neighborhood was developing, it's one of the oldest public gardens in Nice. This peaceful oasis in central Nice was originally called the *Jardin du Roi* in homage to the King of Württemberg, a regular guest before and after the war of 1870. It acquired its current name in 1914 after the Alsace

and Lorraine departments that France lost in 1871 and fought to regain.

Amid the exotic species and the children's playground, the garden is notable for the central water fountain decorated with a sculpture by Antoniucci Volti (1915-1989) *Femme endormie* (sleeping woman). Notice also the monument to Paul Déroulède by Michel de Tarnowsky (1870-1946) and *Main à l'urne* by the Algerian sculptor, Andre Greck (1912-1993), which symbolizes French Algeria.

Turn right onto boulevard Gambetta, go up a block and across the street is

(2) La Rotonde at No 41. Constructed in 1929 by the architect Georges Dikansky (1881-1963), this exuberant Art Deco structure is a historic monument. Dikansky emigrated from Russia in 1911 and created a number of outstanding buildings in Nice. Notice how the facade seems to ripple as the rectangular design gives way to the "rotunda". The polychrome mosaics on the fifth floor recall the sea and the top is adorned with a bas-relief and two gazebos. With its profusion of decorative motifs , the building is a splendid example of early Art Deco style as it developed in Nice.

Retrace your steps, turn left and head up **boulevard Victor Hugo**. The street was laid out in the 1850s and acquired its name in 1885 upon the death of the legendary writer. Lined with plane trees and stately buildings, it's one of the most attractive and prestigious boulevards in Nice. Fenced gardens separate many of the buildings from the sidewalk, a feature that was intended to ornament the public thoroughfare. Most of the buildings date from the beginning of the 20th century and the predominant style is Art Deco.

189

Boulevard Victor Hugo in 1890

Make the first right onto rue Cronstadt to see the

(3) Villa La Belle Epoque at No 18. Now that's a
difference. Built in 1911 before Art Deco buildings became
trendy, the architect was Jean-Baptiste Blanchi (1852-1913).
The star is Michel de Tarnowsky who sculpted the elaborate
frieze just under the winter garden. Next door is the **Villa
Asphodele** an Art Deco jewel.

Return to boulevard Victor Hugo and continue east to
the

(4) Palais Les Mimosas at No 53. Nice architect
René Liviera (1918-1995) masterminded this seven-story Art
Deco building from 1938 and it's a beauty. The distinctive
yellow ocher, brown ocher, gray and aquamarine color
scheme allude to the building's flowery name. Notice the

almond-shaped entrance flanked by columns in a nod to the baroque period and the rounded balconies that recall waves. The hexagons, rotundas and half-cut sides add up to an extraordinarily rhythmic facade.

Onward to No 45 and the

(5) Palais Meyerbeer another masterpiece of the Belle Epoque era and a historic monument. Built in 1908 by the Nice architect Adrien Rey for a Swiss industrialist, Isaac Murisier, the ornamentation is opulent inside and out. Don't miss the frieze of frolicking cherubs on top. There are only six apartments in this massive building which remains among the most prestigious addresses in Nice. The pharmacy on street level has been there since the beginning and is worth a peek inside for its original features.

For a stunning change of decor cross the street and take a look at

(6) Two Art Deco Buildings from the 1930s at nos 36 and 38bis with their clean lines and lack of ornamentation. Although twins, they are painted two different colors for visual interest. The 90° angles are softened with the presence of rounded balconies. Look closely and see how the variety of balconies adds visual interest. Only floors two, three and four are identical; the others are styled differently.

Continue on to the

(7) Palais Marie at No 27, an Art Deco masterpiece by Georges Dikansky built in 1930. The two adjoining

191

buildings are adorned with imposing square turrets on an ornate facade outfitted with moldings, fluted pilasters and stylized ironwork which is a feature of Art Deco style. There's a lot to look at here from the moldings around the balconies to the unusual (for that period) floral motifs that crop up everywhere.

Continue on a block to rue Docteur Baréty. On the corner is the

(8) Eglise Reformé, a Neo-Gothic church built in

1886 to serve the American community in Nice. At first Americans came for their health. Respiratory diseases were on the rise and Nice's fresh sea air seemed like an antidote. Then they came for the social scene. The great families of Vanderbilt, Morgan, Cornell, Hamilton, Gordon-Bennett and Jay Gould were all over the fashionable promenades, cafes and sports events.

The Anglican Church of the Holy Trinity on rue de la Buffa initially served the Americans but conflicts arose and a new church became necessary. The Vanderbilts gave generously to construct the "American Church", focusing on the presbytery, furnishings and church organ.

The American congregation remained numerous enough to support the church through WWII but once the Sixth Fleet departed neighboring Villefranche-sur-Mer, the church began a slow, steady slide. Finally in 1974 the Reformed Church of France took over its functions.

The church is only open for Sunday mass and sundry church events but if you do find yourself inside, note the stained glass windows.

Make a right on rue Docteur Baréty and left on rue Joffre to see the

(9) Palais Baréty at No 31 where we are back to Belle Epoque architecture. Built in 1898 for Dr Baréty, the style is relatively austere compared to other buildings of the time. The use of protruding stone and tinted concrete is an early example of a style that became common in Nice. Oriel windows ornamented with mosaics on the side of the building are a graceful touch. The slender arched windows that seem to descend the facade are part of the stairwell. Certainly the most unique feature are the 50 bull heads supporting the top balcony which is a reminder of the rural origins of the Baréty family. Lucien Barbet was the architect and the building is a historic monument.

Return to boulevard Victor Hugo. Turn left, heading west. Make a right on rue Baquis and then a left on **rue Verdi**. In contrast to the purely residential rue Victor Hugo, rue Verdi has small shops, cafes and boutiques populating the stately buildings. You'll first come to the

(10) Art Deco buildings at nos1 **and 3**. At first glance the buildings seem rather bland but look closely to admire the understated bas-reliefs, the bow windows and the variety of balconies. The wave patterns on the facade and on the cornice between the fifth and sixth floors of No 3 are repeated vertically on the door.

(11) Le Colisée at No 10 is another impressive Art Deco building dating from 1930 and built by the Armenian architects, Kevork Arsenian and Garabed Hovnanian . *Le Clos de Laure* is a small boutique on the ground floor that sells excellent artisanal jams, tapenades and syrups made from local products.

Go on to

(12) Palais Alzira and Palais Amneris at 12

and 14 respectively which were built around 1935. In fact it is one building with two addresses and entrances. The names refer to a Verdi opera composed in 1845 and a lead character in Verdi's opera, *Aida* respectively.

At No 16 a plaque honors

(13) Georges Makowski who lived on the fifth

floor while second in command of the Polish resistance network during the Italian occupation of WWII. On July 6, 1943 he heard police cars stop outside. Knowing what was in store and fearful he would implicate others under torture, the brave Latvian burnt all his documents by the time the carabinieri forced open his door. He then threw himself out the window.

You'll pass rue Berlioz which was a verdant valley until 1909 when work began to cover the valley and create a street. If the 1909 Belle Epoque building at **No 33** looks bizarre it's because the two top floors were added in the 1960s.

Two buildings at the end of the street are truly exceptional. First, admire

(14) La Pergola at No 36 (unknown architect) with its

sumptuously painted facade, carefully restored in 2016. Built in 1926, the Pergola building represents a uniquely *Niçois* Art

Deco style. The "pergola" designs on the first and fifth floors combine blue and yellow coatings using an ancient technique halfway between fresco and sgraffito. Notice the glazed ceramics framing the entrance door, the colored cement coatings on the ground floor and the balustrades, and the ironwork with varying floral motifs.

Go on a short distance to the

(15) Palais Semiramis at No 40, one of the first

constructions from architect Georges Dikansky who created *La Rotonde*. Built in 1928, this highly inventive building combines the grandeur and verticality of Art Deco with the mosaics and floral motifs that often characterize Art Nouveau. Semiramis was the Queen of Babylon and the pergola that crowns the building evokes the Hanging Gardens of Babylon. Note the two imposing oriel windows supported by elegant stylized corbels on building A.

Across the street are the

(16) Franche Comté and Ile de France

buildings at nos 37 and 39. Both are by architect Marcel Delattre and date from around 1939. These late Art Deco buildings display an austere (some say fascistic) style characteristic of the Palais de Chaillot in Paris.

Retrace your steps a short way and make a left on **rue Guiglia** for four contrasting

(17) Art Deco buildings: No 12 is the most

symmetrical. Note how the bow windows rise above the top floor. **No 14** is the most classical. **No 16,** known as *La*

Casamene, is most unusual. Built in the mid-1920s, the architect Nicolas Anselmi displays an innovative use of heavy columns and a large central bay window on the fourth floor to startling effect. **No 18** is beautiful in its simplicity.

Make a right on

(18) rue Rossini

where Art Deco again rules the day. You'll notice that the style of combining protruding stone and tinted concrete is widespread here. Among the series of buildings note: **nos 63 and 65** where the elevator bisects the building; **No 49** dating from 1929; **No 38** with its unique porthole; **No 36,** a 1920s building with an elaborate entrance; **No 30,** also from the 1920s where the ironwork features typical fruit basket motifs.

Take a left on rue Gounod for a dip into Russian history at the

(19) Hotel Oasis

at No 23. At the end of the 19th century the hotel was owned by Mme Vera Krougopoleva and called *La Pension Russe.* Madame gave a discount to her compatriots in the mother country, thus making her establishment the go-to place for Russian visitors and expats. Many came for health reasons as tuberculosis was cutting a lethal swathe through Europe.

Russian playwright Anton Chekhov was one of those people. He was diagnosed with tuberculosis in 1897 and soon after headed to Nice to spend the winter of 1897-1898. Surrounded by Russians and delighted by the Russian cook's borscht, Chekhov received lady friends, worked on stories and letters, followed the news of the day and gambled a little in Monte Carlo. At the end of the winter he left for Russia only to return for the winter of 1900 where he began work on his masterpiece, *Three Sisters*.

Later on, *La Pension Russe* welcomed Lenin who came in 1909 and 1911. "It's splendid here, the dry, hot air, the sea at noon", he wrote to his sister.

Continue up rue Gounod and at the corner of **avenue Clemenceau** on the left is the

(20) Palais Clemenceau at No 34. This

extraordinary Art Deco building dates from 1930. From the wrought-iron doorway to the asymmetrical balconies to the decorative pergola on top, architects Constantin and Cordone did everything to avoid monotony while remaining harmonious. Notice the painted Egyptian motifs displaying papyrus, bamboos and palm trees.

Make a right on avenue Clemenceau and on the right at No 21 is

(21) L'Escurial, a monumental structure that was

considered an architectural jewel. Built by Greek architect Léonard Varthaliti and completed in 1933, the building has a unique facade that's partly circular and topped with a square lantern tower. It was built as a grand cinema, a true temple to the 7th art that only showed the most prestigious films.

The building was brilliantly illuminated at night making it visible from what is now avenue Jean Médecin. The theater itself was inspired by a Greek agora with columns and paintings of classical scenes.

When the age of grand cinemas had passed the building was transformed into a trendy nightclub, *L'Odace*. Over the vociferous objections of traditionalists, the interior was destroyed in 2012 and it became a supermarket. The ironwork at the entrance is new as the original cinema didn't have doors. It now houses small shops.

Backtrack a block and take a right on avenue Durante. Walk until you come to No 19, the

(22) Hotel Excelsior a stately four-star hotel that

was the scene of the greatest atrocities in Nice during WWII. Under the Italian occupation (1940-1943) Nice was a refuge for Jews, both local and those escaping persecution elsewhere. All that changed when the Germans arrived in September 1943. The Austrian SS officer Aloïs Brunner who specialized in rounding up, torturing and deporting Jews, chose the Excelsior as his headquarters because of its proximity to the train station.

It soon became a house of horrors. Brunner supervised a staff of 10 torturers and a handful of medical personnel. Upon arrival detainees were stripped of money and valuables and then subjected to beatings. Forty children were killed with a shot of strychnine. Women and girls were sterilized and sent off to work as sex slaves on the Eastern front.

Brunner's reign of terror only lasted until December 1943 but he managed to send 1820 prisoners to death camps. He probably would have doomed more but for the almost total lack of cooperation from the local populace. The deportations continued after his departure but at a much reduced level. By August 1944 3000 Jews had been sent from Nice to the detention camp of Drancy, near Paris, and then on to Auschwitz. The building was restored and now the only reminder of its sinister history is a plaque across the street.

Continue up avenue Durante, go up the ramp and turn left on avenue Thiers to the

(23) Post Office constructed in 1931 entirely in brick which is unusual for this region. Because this Art Deco masterpiece was such a break with the prevailing style, rumors flew that the red brick building was initially designed for northern France where it seems to belong. But no. Architect Guillaume Tronchet designed it to accommodate Nice's growing population which obviously needed a massive and important-looking post office. It was also highly practical with an ingenious tunnel system that linked the post office to the train station.

The most outstanding feature is the 27-meter-high clock tower, consisting of some 300,000 bricks from Sarzana, Italy. The bricks were cut in various sizes and angles to create visual interest. Don't miss the sculpted figures by Jan and Joel Martel on the eastern side of the building depicting three women in profile. Most of the interior has been redone but it's worth entering to admire the original glass ceiling.

Go in the opposite direction, heading east along avenue Thiers to reach the

(24) Gare Thiers or Nice-Ville train station. It seems fitting to end the walk at the place that sparked the development of the neighborhood. Designed by architect Louis Jules Bouchot, the Louis XIII style was intended to echo the style of Parisian public buildings. It received the first train in 1864 and was completed in 1867, only seven years after Nice became part of France.

The interior had to be fit for the European royalty that were already wintering in the region. The monumental reception hall, dining hall and waiting rooms were festooned with oak paneling, reliefs and stuccoes. In 1865 Tsar Alexander of Russia and the Tsarina were the first royals to set foot in the station, followed by Napoleon III, King Leopold of Belgium, Queen Victoria and many more.

The original building was modernized and extended over the years, most recently in 2014, but the facade, elements of the ceiling and original glass and steel train shed remains. The latest project will connect the train station with avenue Jean Médecin to the east via a glass and metal structure that will feature shops, office spaces, a hotel, an auditorium and a restaurant with a roof terrace.

LA PLUS BELLE SALLE DE LA COTE D'AZUR

NICE - L'ESCURIAL - AV. GEORGES-CLÉMENCEAU
(A 50 mètres de l'Avenue de la Victoire)

QUARTIER DES MUSICIENS MAP

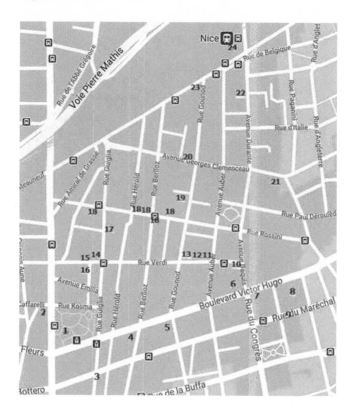

Map Key

1. Alsace Lorraine Garden
2. La Rotonde
3. Villa La Belle Epoque
4. Palais Les Mimosas
5. Palais Meyerbeer
6. Art Deco buildings
7. Palais Marie
8. Eglise Reformé
9. Palais Baréty
10. Art Deco buildings
11. Le Colisée
12. Palais Alzira and Amneris
13. Makowski plaque
14. La Pergola
15. Palais Semiramis
16. Franche Comté and Ile de France
17. Art Deco buildings
18. 63, 49, 38,36,30 Rue Rossini
19. Hotel Oasis
20. Palais Clemenceau
21. L'Escurial
22. Excelsior Hotel
23. Post Office
24. Gare Thiers

BIBLIOGRAPHY

1917, Nice L'américaine: Exposition, Archives De Nice Côte D'Azur, Palais De Marbre, 1er Mars-29 Septembre 2017. Service Des Archives Nice Côte D'Azur, 2017.

Barbarin, Jacques. "Nice, Le Quartier DesMusiciens." *Ciaovivalaculture*, 6 Jan. 2015, ciaovivalaculture.com/2015/01/06/nice-le-quartier-des-musiciens/.

Barelli Hervé, et al. *Vieux-Nice: Guide Historique Et Architectural.* Serre, 1997.

Barelli, Hervé. *Inventaire Du Patrimoine Monumental Et Historique Du Vieux-Nice* . Serre, 1996.

Barelli Hervé, and Roger Rocca. *Histoire De L'identité niçoise.* Serre, 1998.

Benevenuto, Alex. *Guide Amoureux, Secret Et Historique Du Vieux Nice.* Serre, 2013.

Bilas, Charles. *Nice Secret Et Insolite : Les TrésorsCachés De La Baie Des Anges.* Les Beaux Jours. Paris, 2018.

Bouiron, Marc. *Nice, La Colline Du château: HistoiremillénaireD'une Place Forte.* Ville De Nice, 2013.

Boyer, Frédéric, editor. *Les 75 Monuments Historiques De Nice.* MémoiresMillénaire, 2017.

Bruyas, Laure. "L'immeubleNiçoisOù a Vécu Matisse TombeEnRuine ." *Nice Matin*, 16 May 2016.

Cagnoli, Sébastian. "Falicon, Nice." *Falicon, Sainte-Hélène*, ratatoulha.chez-alice.fr/_genealogie/falicon-ste-helene.html.

"Cimiez." *Lou Sourgentin*, June 2011.

"La libération du Pays Niçois" *Lou Sourgentin,* September 2014

"Musique et quartier des musiciens" *Lou Sourgentin,* April 2007

"Histoire d'un Marché aux puces" *Lou Sourgentin,* February 1996

Dallo, Roberte. "Le Béton Coloré : Un Patrimoine Art Déco,
Un Matériaud'Avenir." *La Pierre D'Angle*, Jan. 2018,
anabf.org/pierredangle/magazine/le-beton-color-un-
patrimoine-art-d-co-un-mat-riau-d-avenir.

Gayraud, Didier. *Guide Amoureux, Secret Et Historique Du
Vieux Nice*. Editions De Cabri, 1997.

Geist, Henri, and Henri Bernardi. "Regard Inédit Sur Les
Vestiges De La Forteresse De Nice." *Archéam*, no. 11, 1
Jan. 2004.

Kundahl, George G. *Riviera at War: WWII on the Cote D'Azur*.
I.B. Tauris, 2017.

"La Libération Du Pays Niçois." *Lou Sourgentin*, Sept. 2014.

Levitt, Robert. "Exploring Jewish Nice." *Via Nissa*,
www.vianissa.com/uncategorized/exploring-jewish-nice/.

Levitt, Robert. "Why Has Nice Forgotten the American
President Thomas Jefferson?" *Le Blog De Vieux Nice*,
Nice Matin, 20 Sept. 2019,
leblogduvieuxnice.nicematin.com/2019/09/20/old-nice-
why-has-nice-forgotten-the-american-president-thomas-
jefferson/.

Massimi, Michel. *Cimiez : Promenade Au Fil Du Temps*.
Editions Des Régionalismes. Cressé , 2013.

Moak, David Geoffrey. "Une Ville Des Jardins: The
Consigliod'Ornato and the Urban Transformation of
Nice (1832-1860)." *Journal of Urban History*, vol. 45, no. 4,
2018, pp. 786–812., doi:10.1177/0096144218768499.

Nice Patrimoine. *D'un Monde à L'autre : Les Entrées Des
Demeures Du Vieux-Nice*, Nice Ville, 2008.

Nice Patrimoine. *Le Pont-Vieux, Des Remparts, Et Des
Fouilles Archéologiques*, Nice Ville, 2006.

Nice Patrimoine. *Eau Et Fontaines à Nice*, Nice Ville, 2008.

Nice Patrimoine. *La Colline De Cimiez*, Nice Ville, 2015.

Nice Patrimoine. *La Colline De Fabron*, Nice Ville, 2015.

Nice Patrimoine. *La Place Garibaldi, Un Parfum d'Italie*, Nice
Ville, 2005.

Nice Patrimoine. *La Reine Victoria à Nice*, Nice Ville, 2006.

Nice Patrimoine. *La Tour Bellanda*, Ville De Nice, 2011.

Nice Patrimoine. *Le Consiglio D'Ornato, Créateur D'une Nice
Moderne : 1832-1860*, Nice Ville, 2006.

Nice Patrimoine. *Le Monument Aux Morts*, Nice Ville, 2006.

Nice Patrimoine. *Le Sénat De Nice*, Ville De Nice, 2017.

Nice Patrimoine. *Les Palais Du Vieux-Nice*, Nice Ville, 2018.

Nice Patrimoine. *Les Ports De Nice*, Nice Ville, 2006.

Nice Patrimoine. *L'Opéra De Nice*, Ville De Nice, 2004.

Nice Patrimoine. *Nice Palais Des Rois De Sardaigne Palais De La Préfecture*, Ville De Nice, 2005.

Nice Patrimoine. *Nice The Castle Hill*, Ville De Nice, 2014.

Nice Patrimoine. *Nice's Crypt*, Ville De Nice, 2012.

Nice Patrimoine. *Sur Les Berges Du Paillon, FleuveNiçois*, Nice Ville, 2008.

Nice Patrimoine. *The Chapels of the Penitents Brotherhoods in Nice*, Ville De Nice, 2014.

Nice Patrimoine. *The Churches of Vieux Nice*, Ville De Nice, 2014.

Nice Patrimoine. *The Cruciixion by Brea, a Renaissance*, Ville De Nice, 2014.

Nice Patrimoine. *The Promenade Des Anglais*, Nice Ville, 2005.

Nice Patrimoine. *Un Lieu Du Souvenir : Les Cimetières Du Château De Nice*, Nice Ville, 2005.

Peyregne, Andre. "Quand Le Compositeur Hector Berlioz Se FaisaitRenvoyer Du Comté De Nice Par La Police." *Nice Matin*, 1 Dec. 2019, www.nicematin.com/histoire/quand-le-compositeur-hector-berlioz-se-faisait-renvoyer-du-comte-de-nice-par-la-police-434625.

Pintus, Isabelle. "TourismeAristocratiqueBritannique à Nice Et Sur La Cöte D'Azur." Departement 06.

Pogliano, Richard. *Mystères Et Curiosités De Nice*. Editions Campanile. [Sophia-Antipolis, 2015.

Pogliano, Richard. *Nice Au Coeur Des Quartiers*. Campanile. Sophia Antipolis, 2013.

PSS-Archi.eu. www.pss-archi.eu/.

Rossi, Edmond. *Légendes Et ChroniquesInsolites Des Alpes-Maritimes*. Éditions Des Régionalismes, 2017.

Schor, Ralph. "Les Étrangers Dans La Banlieue De Nice AuCours Des Années 1920." *VillesEnParallèle*, vol. 15, no. 1, June 1990, pp. 208–223., doi:10.3406/vilpa.1990.1084.

"Zoom Sur Carras." *Journal Des Quartiers Carras*, Feb. 2016.

ABOUT THE AUTHOR

Photo by Carmen Blike

Jeanne is a professional travel writer who has been reporting about European destinations regularly since 1996. She has written guidebooks about France, Croatia, Greece, Germany, Slovenia, Belgium and the Netherlands for Lonely Planet, Frommer's and Insight Guides. Her travel articles have appeared in the Miami Herald, San Francisco Chronicle, St Petersburg Times, the Denver Post, National Geographic Traveler and the New York Post.

She now publishes travel websites: croatiatraveller.com, frenchrivieratraveller.com and riviera-beaches.com. Her website, niceuncovered.com provides additional tips, updates, images and a behind-the-scenes look at this book. She has been living in Nice, France since 1999.

INDEX

210

211

Nice's Anthem

Nissa la Bella	Nice la Belle
Viva, viva, Nissa la Bella	Vive, vive, Nice la Belle
O la miéu bella Nissa	O my beautiful Nice
Regina de li blur	Queen of flowers
Li tiéu viehi taulissa	Your old roofs
Iéu canterai always.	I will always sing them.
Canterai li mountagna	I will sing the mountains
Lu tiéu tant ric decor	Your so rich decor
Li tiéu verdi campagna	Your green countryside
Lou tiéu gran soulèu d'or.	Your great golden sun.
Toujou iéu canterai	**I will always sing**
Souta li tiéu tounella	**Under your arbors**
La tiéu mar d'azur	**Your azure sea**
Lou tiéu cièl pure	**Your pure sky**
E toujou griderai	**And always I will sing**
in the miéu ritournella	**In my chorus**
Viva, viva, Nissa la Bella .	**Long live Nice la Belle .**
Canti la capelina	I sing the capeline
La rosa e lou lilà	The rose and the lilac
Lou Pouòrt e la Marina	The Port and the Marine
Paioun, Mascouinà!	Paillon, Mascoïnat!
Canti la soufieta	I sing the attic
Doun birth li cansoun	Where the songs are born
Lou fus, la coulougneta,	The spindle, the distaff
The miéu bella Nanoun.	My beautiful Darling.
Canti li nouòstri gloria	I sing our glories
L'antic e bèu calèn	The ancient and beautiful Roman lamp
Dòu dounjoun li vitoria	The victories of the castle
L'oudou dòu tiéu spring!	The smell of your spring!
Canti lou vielh Sincaire	I sing the old Sincaire
Lou tiéu white drapèu	Your white flag
Pi lou brès of my mayor	Then my mother's cradle
Dòu mounde lou plus bèu.	From the most beautiful world.